Life Pi

www.LifePivot.co.uk

Copyright 2019 Bradley Askew

All rights reserved. No part of this publication may be reproduced, stored in a retrieval system, or transmitted in any form or by any means without the prior permission of the copyright owner.

ISBN: 9781072181750

www.LifePivot.co.uk

Dedicated to Hazel Askew

We have walked and run

Along a twisting path

You are always there

Naughty and fun

Though there are many winters

With you it is always spring

Green buds of life

Hope and love

Acknowledgements

A special thank you to a small group of friends who have helped me on this project. In particular Andrew Mitchell, Ben Spiller and Rob Scott-Cook for reading the first raw manuscript and giving such honest and helpful feedback. A huge thank you to Zahra Spiller for proofreading and editing the book. Thank you Haze for being such a great listener as I have processed these ideas out loud.

I could not have done this alone.

Contents

1. Introduction
2. My Pivot(s)
3. Uniquely Passionate
4. Uniquely Capable
5. Unique Weaknesses and Limitations
6. Unique Personality
7. Uniquely Motivated
8. Unique Coordinates
9. The Process of Change
10. Research and Development
11. Developing your Vision
12. Leaving the Shire

Introduction

"People may spend their whole lives climbing the ladder of success only to find, once they reach the top, that the ladder is leaning against the wrong wall."

Thomas Merton

In 2013, a Gallup poll revealed that for eighty-seven percent of the workforce, work is more often a source of frustration than fulfilment in that workers felt emotionally disconnected from their workplaces.

What can be more important than having self-worth, purpose, and passion in one's life? I am convinced that for the overwhelming majority of us, we do not find what we were put on this planet for in Act One Scene One, but rather much later on in our lives.

We have all had a 'why?' moment at some point but it is hard to find that 'why?' when you are older and patterns of behaviour have become so entrenched. We end up making assumptions about the way things should be. Questions are no longer asked. Options are no longer considered. Reacquainting yourself once again with who you are and what makes you tick is all important.

For most of us, the first half of life is about our 'Darwinian' need to 'survive successfully'. We do what gains us approval from our peers, teachers, role models, parents, and other influential authority figures. We do more and more of whatever causes those around us to say: "So and so has done well."

Such success typically includes getting a job, earning money, finding somewhere to live, buying a car, holding down a significant relationship, becoming parents and perhaps indulging in a holiday abroad now and then. These are all good things and often a necessity but there comes a time in life when we need to scrutinise these extrinsic goals and scripts because we either succeed or fail at them only to discover in the words of an American monk that:

"People may spend their whole lives climbing the ladder of success only to find, once they reach the top, that the ladder is leaning against the wrong wall."

Thomas Merton

This moment of ambiguity and anxiety sets the stage for what I like to describe as a "Life Pivot".

A pivot is a turn or rotation. It is constantly used in entrepreneurial circles to describe what happens when a 'start-up' has followed business Plan A but things simply are not working well. Despite these short comings, there is ample data to wade through and more importantly, to learn from. Based on what the entrepreneur now knows to be true about the reality and the way things work, the opportunity presents itself for him or her to change the game and follow a new and more fruitful trajectory.

This book is about how we can understand ourselves better and follow a new and more fruitful trajectory that mirrors our unique capabilities and passions, weaknesses and limitations, our personality and the often overlooked matter of motivation.

We are all a work in progress, our journeys are utterly unique and we each have vast quantities of 'data' (aka experience) to learn from. There may be dreams you chased that just did not happen for whatever reason, and there may be times you felt more alive than words can describe and you never told a living soul because it sounded childish. Maybe you feared being labelled a 'Walter Mitty', a dreamer, with your head in the clouds.

The front cover of this book reads, *'How do I answer the question, what should I do with the rest of my life?"* In this book I want to share how you might go about answering that question. I will not present simplistic answers but rather I will challenge you to treat your journey like an archaeological dig as I present strategies, tools and guidance on where you might start digging. If the only achievement from you reading this book is to validate the idea that you are meant to flourish by being one hundred percent yourself then I will have done my job.

At this stage it might also be helpful to say that I have zero academic qualifications on this subject. I am not a career counsellor or a psychologist. Rather, I am simply someone who has walked down this road and struggled with these questions.

To quote the famous inventor Thomas A Edison:

"I am more of a sponge than an inventor. I absorb ideas from every source."

I think we all do that. I will draw your attention to many thoughts and wise words I have gleaned from various places which together I hope will form a symphony of wisdom that can help you the way they have helped me.

There are five different questions each having a chapter of their own in the middle of this book. These questions are:

    A. What am I passionate about, (animated and energized by)?

    B. What am I gifted and uniquely capable at (including skills)?

    C. What weaknesses and external limitations exist? (These are just as real and influential as my strengths and opportunities)

    D. What is my basic personality type? (We cannot change our basic personality type)

E. What motivates me? (Motivations change in different seasons)

Each of these questions will help you 'peel the onion' of your true self and uncover the reality of who you are. Be prepared to be surprised as you are far more uniquely capable and passionate than you realise.

If each of these questions were to produce a corresponding set of coordinates for a map, then by the end of this book you will have put yourself onto this map in the form of five clear truth statements. Drawing a line through those five points on the map should provide you with the direction you are seeking.

In public spaces like zoos we find large maps. The first thing the visitor does is search for the words 'You are Here'. Without knowing that the map is useless. In this book I hope to help you position yourself on a map of sorts by seeing yourself as you really are (warts and all).

Perhaps you have picked up this book because you feel there is more to you than your current job or situation offers, or there are seeds of something deep down inside of you that you are yearning to release but you do not know where to start.

I have written this book because I am convinced that human beings are designed to flourish. And, when we flourish those around us also flourish and the ripple effect on the world around us is immeasurable.

My Pivot(s)

It is only fair I share a little about my own journey if only to show you that this book exists not because I have found pivoting in life easy but rather because it has been an area of great struggle. Trying to answer that question, 'what should I do with the rest of my life?' has been tough.

Although we are human beings and not human doings, every morning most people wake up, shower, eat their breakfast and go off somewhere to do something and hopefully that "something" is meaningful for them and those they love. I once knew what that 'thing' was for me. But with the passage of time and change in me and my circumstances, the meaning became somewhat opaque.

I worked as a civil and commercial lawyer in a national law firm in England for about seven years. That work involved representing individuals who had suffered financial harm mostly because of a breach of contract. This in turn resulted in the opportunity to lead a small team of other lawyers and also to do advocacy. I enjoyed it.

But by about 2007 I realised that whilst I had flourished at a junior level I had colleagues who were so much more passionate about their craft than me and they seemed to love their work. They eagerly awaited the outcome of Court of Appeal cases and seemed far more aspirational than I was. Even then I realized there is a definite correlation between how much one loves what one does and how well one does it.

My first life pivot was into becoming a legal entrepreneur. Given my background in law, I wanted to help people access legal help via the internet. The internet had disrupted lots of things but not the law. There were price comparison sites for car insurance, last minute holiday's but law seemed to me to remain in the pre-internet age.

Legal issues are often upsetting and stressful. Legal problems can include a loss of employment, health, a family member, housing, or risk to business and loss of jobs or income. At the time people could only access legal advice if they had the money or legal insurance. I had a big dream and over the course of four years, I gathered an exceptional team, and we built an exceptional online legal brand which became one of the biggest legal websites in the UK and it helped people find the right legal advice and the best thing was that most of that guidance was free.

Starting a business was a pipe dream of sorts in that I knew the odds were against me, and that I was attempting to do something that for most people ended in tears. Did you know that eighty percent of start-ups fail within the first twelve months and of the twenty percent that survive only half of those exist five years later?

I had a conviction it was a risk worth taking because it had the potential to help people, plus my main motivation was that my eldest son Barny was just one at the time. I was desperate to have autonomy over my diary so that I could be a more present husband and father. Running a business presented more challenges than I care to write about. In fact, there were many days when it felt like I was stepping into a boxing ring, but a combination of incredible people, sheer determination and what felt like a miracle, the enterprise flourished and we not only survived but also thrived.

If I am honest with you, I had not thought ahead to what would happen next. I was focused on the here and now and was giving my undivided attention to the simple notion of survival. Like most entrepreneurs, I suffered from 'impostor syndrome' and deep down did not think I would succeed anyhow. It felt like I wanted to summit Everest when I had never even been hill walking. Everest is a dangerous enterprise, and the vision is to reach the summit but one never really thinks much about what happens after that goal of reaching the top. All the mental energy is about ascent. In fact, most injuries happen on the descent.

In 2011 a large German-owned insurance company wanted to acquire my business.

The deal had been in process for about six months. The first meeting with the buyer involved a normal trading relationship and then it dawned on them how we had created something of real value and very special: A portal with tens of thousands of people coming through it each year, with the need for a lawyer in one area of law or another. That realisation led to further lunches and then a process through which we eventually sold the business. That felt like the aforementioned summit experience and what I suppose every entrepreneur dreams of. To have a large and well established company, state in ways that matter that they love what you have built is both validating and affirming.

I remember the law firm table was about thirty feet long and legal documents lined the circumference. The share purchase agreement, stock transfer forms, Companies House filings, a deed of contribution, and about thirty other documents all in triplicate. We had been there since ten am and it was now ten pm and we were growing weary. The final tweaks to the completion mechanism were in black and white, and we needed signatures. Lots of them.

I was the founder and owner of the business for sale but for everyone else in that room (lawyers, accountants, and directors), it was probably less impactful on a personal level; just another day at the office.

The time came to sign the paperwork, and we moved around the large table in a clockwise direction signing document after document. At that point, someone declared the deal to be 'complete'. Most people went home and about five of us went to the local pub on Victoria Street for a pint. What an anti-climax. I was being asked: "How do you feel Brad?" "What next for you Brad?" All I could think of was getting a good night's sleep and then turning up for work the next day.

My corporate advisor told me that everything would change and that as much as I tried to continue to lead entrepreneurially, my role would shift from deciding to recommending; the new owners would bring a bigger strategy and canvas on which they wanted to paint. This turned out to be correct. It felt like I was no longer an entrepreneur and had become an employee. For anyone in this position you will know exactly what I mean.

I had developed an identity in being the company leader, the founder, the one who colourfully described the vision and why what we did mattered. But after selling my business that inevitably changed. It was a bittersweet journey. On the one hand, taking my business from vision to exit was an emotional high, but it also left me unsure about where I fitted into things and what now?

I continued for some time but they had ample talent, resource, and strategies so we amicably agreed that I would move onto new pastures.

Day one after leaving the business I founded was strange to say the least. Suddenly it was quiet. No emails or meetings. No third quarter figures or risk registers. No vision casting with colleagues which I always loved. We would go to Starbucks and I would describe what I saw in my mind's eye: "Wouldn't it be amazing if……..?" All great innovations started like that. It was energizing and exciting and I absolutely loved connecting vision with talent and then sitting back to see what happened next.

But silence. The phone stopped ringing. Do not get me wrong, I immensely enjoyed going for walks and drinking tea with my best friend and wife Haze. But the main things I remember going through my head were "Who am I now? What do I do now?' Both a need to be busy but equally a sense of responsibility to contribute to the world around me, made me feel restless.

A mentor of mine told me to carve out six months (at least) to do nothing at all. The thinking was that I probably needed to 'de-tox' from the corporate world to reflect.

I once spoke with a well-known musician who was part of a world-famous band and he shared with me about his difficulties and bouts of depression that happened after their band hit the big time. Their roaring success was painful. It may sound strange (maybe not), but dreams drive us. After they achieved their goal there was an emptiness.

Our unfulfilled challenges can inspire us with hope and create a certain spring in our step and energize our life. Work creates a dependency on people and it forges strong friendships even amid those struggles. The musician said every personal ambition and dream he had cultivated since an early age (fame, fortune, and creative legacy), was very quickly realised within a period of about one year and that was depressing because without the dream, he felt he had lost his identity.

Who and what are we when we are not achieving something? We are so defined by what we do. At social gatherings, people rarely ask what car you drive, or which town you were born in but they ask those four little words "What do you do?" hoping to determine the social hierarchy around them. It is as if that question really means "who are you and are you worth talking to?"

I was physically and mentally exhausted from building the business and the stress surrounding the deal itself. I think entrepreneurs romanticize certain aspects of their journey like the times they could not pay their own salary but paid everyone else's for example. That really happened. But the reality is it was hard and with that hindsight, it is only human to feel reluctant to enter the same environment again even when armed with the expertise and experience to do so. Stress is stress.

As I reflected, it felt like I was no longer 'employee' material having been self-employed as an entrepreneur for so long, and I felt I lacked the emotional and mental reserves to start something again. That person just did not feel like the true crisp me anymore. I had changed.

That said, there were many possibilities but it felt like they came from the world around me rather than from my heart.

They included:

Becoming a serial entrepreneur.

Everyone says people who start something once cannot stop. Elon Musk famously sold PayPal for $400million and immediately founded Tesla, then SpaceX, and now the Boring Company and Hyperloop. In terms of scale, he is one in a billion but the point is there is an expectation that if you have done something well before, do it again…..and again. There is an expectation you will keep doing whatever you have done well at. We are pattern following creatures. But what if the current or old pattern does not fully express who you are on the inside?

Being a Social Entrepreneur

I spent much time grappling with this. The idea was to take my entrepreneurial skills and experience and start something more social and even charitable. There are wonderful examples of people doing exactly this like Tom's Shoes. It is a profitable business that gifts a pair of shoes to someone without shoes in the developing world every time they sell a pair of shoes in America and Europe. Another example would be my friend Neil Dennison who founded Urban Pursuit (www.urbanpursuit.co.uk) in Bristol as an alternative education provider for children at risk of exclusion from schools.

Investing in other entrepreneurs

I have done this five or six times with mixed results. The main challenge I soon learned is that I am a reluctant leader so putting myself in the back seat of the car when really I am a better driver than a passenger, is a recipe for friction.

Support people in a purely *Pro Bono* manner

This has been and will be forever something that makes sense because I would have accomplished little or nothing without people being there alongside me. I continue to spend between ten and fifteen hours a week meeting with people without any agenda other than to be helpful and encouraging. However, in the world of start-ups and business generally it is a complicated area; it can be human nature not to value that which is free. There is a tension to be managed here.

These are all ideas I explored and participated in and not one of them is ridiculous or unrealistic, but, as we will come to explore later in this book they are all borne out of scripts. By scripts I mean mental maps as to how things are supposed to work. Before you drive from one place to another you visualise the route you will take and then that plays out in reality. The same is true of how we navigate life. We have a mental map or script which guides us in terms of what we should so, how we should do it, and the reasons for that. The problem for me is that some of the 'scripts' were incorrect or outdated and would grate against my actual gifts, passions, skills, weaknesses, limitations, personality, and new motivations.

Using a TomTom analogy, (the GPS Navigation device that we stick to our windscreens), sometimes we need to download fresh maps. The rest of this book, I hope, will help you to do that.

Uniquely Passionate

"There is no passion to be found playing small - in settling for a life that is less than the one you are capable of living." Nelson Mandela

Most people I talk to know what their skills are. That should be readily discoverable by reading one's own LinkedIn profile. You are a solicitor, accountant, strategist, biochemist, full-time parent, a physics teacher and the skills required to do what you have been doing are clearly defined whether that be the ability to communicate, write, educate, combine molecules to create inorganic compounds etc. But, understanding your unique gifts and passions can be much harder to glean.

Do you know what you were born naturally gifted at?

Do you know what you are passionate about?

Most people I talk to cannot answer these two questions.

Put the kettle on and take five minutes now to try honestly answering these two questions using the statements below.

A. The thing I 'get' and can do effortlessly and I would say I am uniquely capable at is……………………………………………..

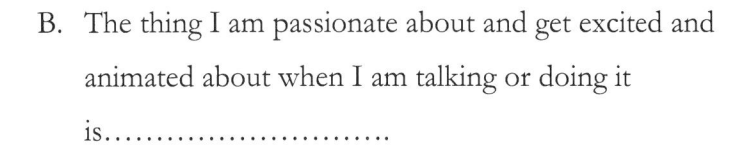

B. The thing I am passionate about and get excited and animated about when I am talking or doing it is………………………….

If you have answered these questions, you're in the minority. But, even if you have answered them I want to politely suggest that you may have given a clear and compelling answer but one that is not entirely true for you on a heart level.

The fact you are reading this book means there is a good chance you have been doing the same thing for quite a long time. You may not even remember how you got to where you are. It is what it is. Maybe you cannot recall how you ended up doing what you are doing. Or maybe you remember the chronology of it all but you do not remember anyone ever having a 'what makes you tick?' conversation with you before you ended up on what now seems like a pre-destined train line taking you to a destination you never knowingly asked to go to. Does this sound familiar?

If such a conversation were to have taken place in your early years, your teacher may have asked you: What makes you laugh? What makes you cry? What makes you angry? What did you absolutely love doing as a child? Which problem in the world would you love to solve and are you willing to educate yourself in school and beyond to enable you to solve that problem?

These would have been great questions for us to have been asked in an ideal world and may have steered our life ships in different trajectories. I think part of the problem lies within our educational systems which are built around a standardised and not personalised approach to learning.

In his book, The Element: How Finding Your Passion Changes Everything, Ken Robinson, eloquently describes the above problem.

"The fact is that given the challenges we face, education doesn't need to be reformed -- it needs to be transformed. The key to this transformation is not to standardize education, but to personalize it, to build achievement on discovering the individual talents of each child, to put students in an environment where they want to learn and where they can naturally discover their true passions." And, *"Imagination is the source of every form of human achievement. And it's the one thing that I believe we are systematically jeopardizing in the way we educate our children and ourselves."*

The point is not that we want the future generations to look more like Peter Pan than Albert Einstein, rather we each flourish more when our own individual design is given room to shape our life paths.

By developing a deep understanding of your "what makes you tick?" I believe it is possible to avoid becoming yet another dissatisfied and emotionally disconnected statistic. This is not a good place to be and there is an alternative.

One of the problems is that we often manufacture compelling answers to important questions.

I was once representing someone in a court case and in assessing the evidence given, the judge said, *'Reconstruction has replaced recollection. You do not appear to remember what happened, so you have reconstructed in your mind what you think happened"*. I suggest we all do that more often than we care to admit.

The author of The Knowledge Illusion: Why We Never Think Alone, (Riv) Sloman's research focuses on judgment, decision-making, and reasoning. He describes it as "the illusion of explanatory depth." And our tendency to over-estimate our understanding of how the world works.

"The decisions we make, the attitudes we form, the judgments we make, depend very much on what other people are thinking," he said.

This explains why we like to fill in the gaps with 'convenient preferred answers' and therefore in this book we are taking a more forensic approach to answer these meaningful questions.

What are you uniquely passionate about?

"There is no passion to be found playing small - in settling for a life that is less than the one you are capable of living." Nelson Mandela

Passion: Passion is caused by strong feelings or beliefs. Synonyms include: ardent, zealous, heartfelt, animated, energetic, raging, burning;

What burns inside you? I have heard it said until you have found a cause you would die for; you have yet to find something you will live for. What causes make you angry, happy, emotional and sad? None of these promises an answer, but they are a good place to start looking.

The famous writer Nicholas Sparks wrote:

"The saddest people I've ever met in life are the ones who do not care deeply about anything at all. Passion and satisfaction go hand in hand, and without them, any happiness is only temporary, because there is nothing to make it last."

And similarly Joseph Hill Whedon, the American screenwriter, director, producer, comic book writer, and composer writes:

"Passion. It lies in all of us. Sleeping... waiting... and though unwanted, unbidden, it will stir... open its jaws and howl. It speaks to us... guides us. Passion rules us all. And we obey. What other choice do we have? Passion is the source of our finest moments. The joy of love... the clarity of hatred... the ecstasy of grief. It hurts sometimes more than we can bear. If we could live without passion, maybe we'd know some kind of peace. But we would be hollow. Empty rooms, shuttered and dank. Without passion, we'd be truly dead." (Buffy the Vampire Slayer, 1998) Joss Whedon

So above we see two interesting perspectives. I am especially drawn to the strong words of Joss Whedon because it undoes the notion that passion is just the feel good factor and a feeling of delight linked to the release of serotonin in the brain. Passion can equally be birthed out of anger, pain, grief and sorrow. It is, simply put, the bit about us that leans forward and says 'this really matters'. It can matter for many reasons.

I cannot read Whedon's words without thinking about some extraordinary humanitarian movements which were birthed not out of joy and delight but out of a place of grief and sorrow that came from witnessing injustice.

We have been privileged in getting to know a charity based in South Africa called Hands at Work, www.handsatwork.org, that works with orphans and widows. They have pioneered a sustainable community based care model which empowers the carers in the community. The founders George and Carolyn describe how passion stirred and then howled to them, (to borrow the words of Joss Whedon).

George and Carolyn Snyman were a seemingly ordinary, white, middle-class couple who started their young married life in a leafy suburb of Pretoria, South Africa's capital, at the height of the Apartheid era. "We just wanted to live a normal life," George says. Both George and Carolyn had what they describe as a conversion experience of God bursting into their lives and "Everything changed in our lives," George remembers. "The way we viewed money, our friends, our time. Everything changed." Carolyn testifies to George's metamorphosis: "He couldn't drive past people standing on the side of the road. He would often bring all sorts of people off the streets home with him. People he'd passed on his way home from work."

At around this time, George met a black pastor named Hezekiah from Hillbrow, the inner city of Johannesburg. Together they visited black townships on weekends. George was exposed to a great deal of suffering amongst the poor. Faced with this reality, George and Carolyn started grappling with what it meant to be a Christian in an affluent, white suburb whilst simultaneously so much hardship was unfolding in South Africa's marginalised townships. "I learned the names of the people dying and it became personal to me. They told me their stories and fears. All I could do was cry with them and pray for them. Of course, I also buried them all. There was a time when we had no money and I buried people in blankets".

The above is the real story around the birth of Hands at Work. I encourage you to visit their website and find out more.

So many of our well known charitable organisations on this planet trace their origins to people who stumbled upon something that required a response and then eventually an entirely new trajectory in life. What is clear to me from this story, is that George and Carolyn did not sit at home talking about their 'what ifs?' but they left their comfort zone and connected with other people who could help them turn that initial spark into something more.

The big question for me has been whether some people are passionate and have an innate capacity to live passionately and care deeply about things but sadly others are not born passionate and need to live a more mediocre and emotionally disconnected life. Passion in this context is not to be confused with different extrovert personality types; still waters can run very deep. I know several people who are rather quiet but have a fire in their eyes.

There are clearly people who have always known what burned within them. Take, for example, the stereotypical ice sculptor who proclaims "I saw the block of ice and just knew that I had to turn it into a horse or other complex mammal and that is what I will spend the next thirty years of my life doing".

There are musicians, athletes and engineers who just knew from an early age that they were drawn to a particular path.

The best example I can think of is the famous artist and comic who always loved doodling in class and created ironic cartoons for his own amusement. It was always there and sure enough, his name is Matt Groening the man behind 'The Simpsons'.

But, I suggest for most of us passions are in fact something we usually discover in seed form, and then we nurture, water, mix with other things until it grows into a tree, or even an orchard. The seeds probably begin as no more than a curiosity or an interest or even an annoyance but over time and with our collaboration, grow into something far bigger.

Perhaps we can become passionate in a similar way to falling in love with someone. There might be an initial interest birthed out of a mutual hobby and physical attraction, and that then leads to a cup of coffee and then over time it can grow into a lifelong loving commitment based on knowing and being known.

Passions can therefore begin as something as cold as a sense of duty but develop into curiosity and then dedication and over time a full-blown fascination.

I draw your attention to this if you are someone who cannot point to an all-encompassing passion in the here and now but you can probably, with the help of friends, identify the seeds of passion in your life.

We were recently in London at the steps to the National Gallery overlooking Trafalgar Square and there were some street performers. We listened to a classically trained violinist playing Coldplay and we were transfixed. The thing that caught my attention even more than the music was the way different people responded. We were there for at least forty-five minutes and I observed the way people behaved.

There were pedestrians who from the other side of the road paused and listened even though their view was blocked by the passing red double-decker buses. Then there were people who took the next step and crossed over to take a photo or short video to no doubt post on Instagram. Then there were those who moved even closer and put their phones away and bags down and wanted to just listen up close. This inner circle was engaging differently. Some were tapping a foot, some rocking side to side and then there was one gentleman I will never forget who had his eyes closed, head bowed and his arms were waving. He was dancing like a child, as if no one was even watching.

I share this story because it mirrors how the seeds of passion probably work in real life. Something gets your attention and you feel an urge to move closer.

Is not this more the case rather than the individuals who were born Mozarts or Roger Federers? I think this is how George and Carolyn candidly describe their journey. Without a doubt, something or in their case someone, grabbed their attention but then the next leg of their journey involved tiny steps in one direction.

It is possible that your true passions have been hidden and out of sight for a long time. I found the question, what am I passionate about, hard to answer. I listed things I thought I was passionate about in my moleskin notebook, and there was a lengthy list (everything from travel, supporting friends, to horticulture and creating entrepreneurial solutions to problems) but so many of the items were things I thought I ought to be passionate about or seemed logical based on my journey rather than things that really moved me on a heart level. This is a process of moving away from being an echo to finding your own voice.

There are two steps I have found to be useful in uncovering passion. The first is to look for the obvious 'trees' (to use the seed analogy) because for some people it may lie waiting in plain sight. The second step is to look for the 'seeds' of passion which can grow into something bigger.

At this point I would like to invite you to engage with a short but profound exercise:

Gather together a small group, or as I did send a WhatsApp message to four to five people whom you trust and know you and have observed you up close.

Ask them: *What do you think I am passionate about?*

Caution. Please insist they ignore what you say you are passionate about and ask them to just share their honest view based on the way you live your life and the themes that seem to come up again and again. When have they seen a sparkle in your eye whilst you are talking? When have they seen you animated, leaning forward in a conversation and behaving like it meant more to you than to other people?

Second, dig deeper on your own. Here are some great questions to spur you on:

1. *What subject could I read one hundred books about without getting bored?*

2. *What could I do for three years even if I were not*

3. *If I won £100m on the lottery how would I spend my time (and that money)?*

4. *Who do I most envy for the work/stuff they get to do, and what about it inspires me?*

5. *What did I love doing as a child? (Before the pressure to pass exams took over)*

6. *Which things have made me angry and motivated me to do something for someone else?*

Finally, with the help of your friends and/or mentor try to complete this sentence:

I have felt most alive and animated on the inside when I ……………..

Uniquely Capable

You just have to find that thing that's special about you that distinguishes you from all the others, and through true talent, hard work, and passion, anything can happen. Dr Dre

What are you good at? What are you uniquely great at? What is it you 'get' more than other people? This has become known in our cultures as a gift or talent and this is one of the five markers we will use to help you understand your true self and identify a path so that what you do next in life is in harmony with who you are.

A gift is a natural ability or talent. Synonyms include flair, aptitude, capacity, endowment, brilliance, dexterity, artistry.

Skills matter but for the purpose of digging deeper, I want to suggest that gifts and passions are of greater importance in you finding your 'why?'

Skills are the ability to do something well. Synonyms include: Experience, readiness and know how.

Either you have certain skills or you do not. It does not matter whether I am passionate about heart surgery. Without the skills and the permission of a senior cardiologist or the General Medical Council, it is unlikely they will allow me to operate. The same could be true of flying, quilting, joinery, or whatever else.

What is it you have gained skills in? This is likely to be through nurture rather than nature. You may have been on courses, read books, and performed a particular role under someone excellent at something and their know-how has rubbed off on you.

Skills are, however, less important in this book because they will not help you answer your deeper 'why?' question. And this book is more about 'why' than 'how'. Also, it is easier to acquire new skills than to change one's nature.

Again, what do you do that comes so naturally, it annoys other people? What is it you do that feels effortless? What is it you have done in your life where your first attempt was probably better than another person's fifth attempt? We are all the best at something.

The challenge in identifying your true gifts/brilliance is that there is a script we follow which comes from various places. We often answer this question based on what we think will gain us approval from those we respect rather than based on the raw, true, crisp version of ourselves.

One such individual who found his 'sweet spot' is a man by the name of Ray Kroc who after World War One started selling paper cups and milkshake machines. He thought his gift was sales. It sort of was but sometime later he met the owners of a new type of restaurant who were making food quickly to be eaten outside of the restaurant and it fascinated him and could somehow understand how the factory like efficiency could have a broad impact elsewhere. This man became the first CEO of McDonalds which today boasts some 8000 restaurants worldwide. He was not the founder or creator but his gift (aged fifty-three) was his ability to spot the explosive trend and communicate that vision to would be franchisees.

Another such example is J K Rowling. By 1993, at the age of twenty-eight, after a very short-lived marriage and hitting rock bottom as a penniless single mother she said "I still had an old typewriter and a big idea".

That big idea was given space to breathe. It turns out that the thing we know J K Rowling for now, is an extraordinary imagination and the ability to tell stories that children and their parents alike want to read. I wonder how many people reading this have had big ideas, but they were dismissed out of hand?

Why is it that some people seem to find that unique talent that sets them on the right course and others do not? I would suggest that part

This idea is set out in far more detail in a book 'Falling Upward', by Richard Rohr. In it, he states that in the first half of our lives we have a goal to survive successfully. This includes financial success, creating relationships, holidays, a house, family, etc. These 'successes' are things our culture approves of and as surely as night follows day, we replicate what those around us most celebrate. We do more of what gains others' approval. Therefore, I suggest an honest answer to this question is harder than it first seems. We have so many filters through which certain ideas cannot get through.

This means many of the things you have become excellent at may differ from other gifts and talents in you that lie dormant waiting to be awakened.

Richard Rohr suggests in his book that the second half of life is less about what we do, but who we are becoming. It is about moving from success to significance and it is a search for significance and fruitfulness which emanates not from us performing well but from living out of our true heart. A different script and paradigm altogether.

History is full of examples of individuals who have lived one way thinking they were doing what they were good at until one day they had what can only be described as an epiphany moment. They suddenly experienced a moment where everything comes together and everything just works.

of the problem is that we do not always know where to look and have a very narrow and limited view of what makes up a special capability.

Let me expand: We are all born with phenomenal capabilities of intelligence, both intellectual and emotional, intuition, imagination as well as a host of other things. But there are obstacles. First, the thing that makes us 'fly' may not fit in any one camp, but rather it might be a combination of many things. For Matt Groening, the genius behind the Simpsons, he was not a gifted politician, artist or comic but when his amusement of these things combined, the result was one of the most widely viewed funny cartoons, filled with political irony poking fun at the issues of the day. He could have said: "I am no Martin Luther King (politician), no Picasso, (artist) and no Michael McIntyre (comic)" but his artistic freedom allowed him to be unique and to create something unique.

Our inability to see how our various capabilities and various types of intelligence fit together holistically means there are possibilities we simply do not consider.

Another important point to make when we reflect on our past experiences is not to assume that everything until now has been a mishap. No. Focus in on the things that went very well. You may see some trends where you have been repeatedly 'lucky' but in truth it was not luck at all.

Understand why some things worked well for you. If you are blessed with unique capabilities then it is altogether likely that your uniqueness came into play in your past triumphs. It was not fairy dust. It was you. What was it about you, the way you thought, the way you behaved and the way you processed information that was unique to you?

Sir Paul McCartney never liked music at school. He found it boring. In fact, Sir Paul applied to join the choir of Liverpool Cathedral but was turned down for lack of a good singing voice. In this story, Sir Paul McCartney knew that he liked music, just not what he was being spoon-fed at school. He therefore decided to write music he did like with his friends John Lennon, George Harrison and later Ringo Starr to create the music he liked. They went on to sell over 178 million albums.

The second reason for the veil over our latent capabilities and talents is that we have over defined what constitutes a worthy talent and gift as part of our educational system. That definition is largely linked to what is of economic benefit in an industrial era. It is therefore still hard for you and for me to think of our gifts outside of the school curriculum in terms of maths, science, the English language, and the humanities. These are certainly necessary for whatever we want to do but for many, our particular unique capability may be less obvious.

In this book, I am inviting you to be open-minded and try to find out when and where it is/has been that you have just been on autopilot and been able to function at a high level in a way that actually brings you energy and energises others. That place is hard to identify because you will take it for granted as it is effortless for you.

I am an 'ideas person'. I have two to three ideas a day (not all good.) and I sometimes write them down but usually I do not because I view them as quite obvious. But not everyone thinks the same way. I therefore find myself in my 'sweet spot' when I am helping someone overcome a problem. I find my mind brainstorming without permission and before I realise it, I have plotted three or four solutions in every direction and it is incredibly visual for me, so much so, that I can draw what I see. Part of this is why I am teased by friends and past colleagues about my unnecessary large number of analogies. I think in pictures and can see the relationship between different things and can imagine what happens if you combine this idea with that idea.

In the context of mentoring other entrepreneurs for me it often looks a bit like a game of 'Boggle'. I like to listen and understand and then shake the idea's core ingredients around and see what other words we can make with the same letters. I then present a novel idea and suggest an entirely different application for what has already been created. Same DNA different context. Or, for the sake of an analogy here, it is like me going through someone else's pantry and then suggesting what else they could bake using the same ingredients. Even in writing this paragraph I have been leaning forward and typing more quickly than usual. This is what our 'sweet spot' does for us. When have you felt that?

My friend Rob is a social worker and supports people with mental health problems. It is heart-warming to know that there are people like him caring for some of the most vulnerable people in our society. But, for half the week Rob also develops properties. Caring for people is absolutely who he is, but there is another side to him which is buying derelict two bedroom houses and restoring and transforming them into five bedroom family homes. When I look at the property at the beginning, I fear that he has bitten off more than he can chew but then as we walk around it he describes what he sees in his mind's eye down to the very details of how light will enter and bounce around the atrium to how certain right angles will give definition to the end of one space and the beginning of another. He visualises how a home will be created allowing a family to enjoy a space together without overcrowding. He uses phrases like 'bring the outside, inside'. He is in his zone. Is he a builder? No. Is he an architect? No. What is it that makes him animated and energized? I would say it is his unique capability to dream and imagine different possibilities and outcomes in his head and then enjoy the process of transformation through a plan of action. Some might see his two jobs as a dichotomy but they actually have something in common –restoration, imagination and the desire to see something or someone get better through a well-managed plan.

I hope the above examples have resonated with you on some level and got you thinking.

Getting practical

First I recommend you find four to five people in your life (who you trust and who you feel know you quite well). Simply ask them what it is that they think you are uniquely good and capable at? And again, a caution, be quite clear that you expect them to speak honestly and ignore whatever you have told them in the past. Ask them to say what they see.

And then do your best to put it into a sentence.

The thing I just 'get' and seem to be uniquely capable at is……………………

Second, here are a few other questions you might ask yourself as a way of digging a bit deeper.

A. What do you enjoy doing even when no one is looking or asking?
B. What is it that once you get started people have to drag you away from?
C. When do you feel so 'in the moment' that several hours can pass and it only feels like a few minutes?
D. What would you do for free if you could?
E. When you are at the airport and go into a newsagent, which magazines do you pick up to read?
F. What do you enjoy talking about?
G. What do you enjoy watching on TV and why?
H. When, at school, did you do incredibly well at something? Projects, organizing things etc. Name two to three and what do they have in common and what was it that you brought to the table that made it a success?

The main point I have tried to get across in this section is that understanding what it is that you 'get' is unlikely to be something you will find in a report card or within a LinkedIn profile. It is something far more nuanced - not just what you are gifted at but the reason for that giftedness and that is about all of you as a person.

Unique Weaknesses and Limitations

"My life is not only about my strengths and virtues; it is also about my liabilities and my limits, my trespasses and my shadow"

Parker J Palmer

We live in a can-do world. After breaking his back, Bear Grylls, reached the summit of Everest. Richard Branson starting an airline because he could not find a good flight home from the Caribbean, and JK Rowling, in the clasp of relative poverty, wrote the Harry Potter classics and became one of the wealthiest women in the UK.

We love stories of such courageous endeavour especially when it is against the odds. If they can do it maybe we can? I would be a hypocrite were I to deny that my own life involved more "against the odds" projects than is healthy. There have been so many things I have achieved mainly because people told me I could not. These included: public speaking (I am rather shy believe it or not, so shy I could not even say my name during the register when I was at school), becoming a solicitor, starting a business, and as you can see even writing.

For me, the words 'you can't' are like a red flag to a bull because I resent limitations; I believe in the power of human ingenuity. In fact, at school, my careers adviser told me I was not a 'high flyer' and that I should aim much lower. I have regularly knowingly defied reality in order to achieve things.

One of my favourite quotes is from the Irish playwright George Bernard Shaw:

"The reasonable man adapts himself to the world; the unreasonable man persists in trying to adapt the world to himself. Therefore, all progress depends on the unreasonable man."

I cite my own experiences because perhaps, like me, in order to achieve things you've always wanted, you have had to be 'unreasonable' and have overcome, persevered, taken unacceptable risks and done things you are not good at, and 'winged it' a little.

At this stage I will introduce an idea that has helped me enormously:

"My life is not only about my strengths and virtues; it is also about my liabilities and my limits, my trespasses and my shadow. An inevitable though often ignored dimension of the quest for "wholeness" is that we must embrace what we dislike or find shameful about ourselves and what we are confident and proud of."

Parker J. Palmer, Let Your Life Speak: Listening for the Voice of Vocation

It is essential for you to spend much time and reflection listing your gifts and passions. It is important to know your unique personality. These are guiding lights on your road ahead without a doubt. But you must become equally comfortable with your weaknesses and limitations.

In this chapter I use the word 'weakness' to refer to internal flaws, character traits, struggles and blind spots. For example, being impatient) And I use the word 'limitations' to refer to external frontiers such as caring for a parent with dementia, or other external realities which shape what you can and cannot do.

I was on a two-day retreat in Salcombe, England and read the above words by Parker Palmer. It was wisdom passed onto him by an elderly lady. The nub of what she said to him was that we spend so much time looking back over our lives, at what has happened, which doors have opened, and which opportunities have fallen into our laps. But we rarely look at what has not happened. Which doors have been slammed in our faces and which negative themes exist including failures of every shape and size?

When I examined my true nature including my weaknesses, they were every bit as much a guiding light as my gifts and passions and to ignore them would cause me to go against the grain of my soul and probably end up frustrated, anxious and maybe even hurting people.

We are surrounded by things we could do, but it is wise to learn to say 'No' and recognize the difference between 'could' and 'should'.

Remember, the helpful wisdom of Richard Rohr in the earlier chapter, a Franciscan Monk, who said the first half of our life is defined by the need to survive successfully. Survival of the fittest. No room for failure or deficiencies. We do more and more of the things that gain the approval of those we respect. It may be hard to hear but we are imperfect. We have blind spots and character flaws.

There are also things we simply cannot do due to external limitations. If you are married with a young family then that is both a blessing and a limitation. Working 75 hour weeks and spending much time away from the family home may prove detrimental to those you love. This is reality and we ignore these facts at our peril.

I expect you will find this part of self-examination difficult because you may feel programmed to be successful and a 'winner'. This is also counter intuitive because statistically you will spend about two hours today on Facebook, LinkedIn, WhatsApp, Instagram or Snapchat looking at the successful images your network post online. You (and I) have a deeply ingrained cognitive bias to be more aware of strengths than weaknesses. In fact, did you know there is in-depth research that we all estimate our own abilities to be greater than they really are?

In psychology (not my field), the Dunning–Kruger effect is a cognitive bias in which people with low abilities overestimate their abilities. Without unpacking these fascinating studies they say it takes a certain level of competence to recognize one's own incompetence. If I were abrupt or bad with people, it would take a certain amount of emotional intelligence and self-awareness to even appreciate I am bad with people. See the problem?

The philosopher Confucius (551–479 BC), said,

"Real knowledge is to know the extent of one's ignorance"

The playwright William Shakespeare (1564–1616), said,

"The fool doth think he is wise, but the wise man knows himself to be a fool" (As You Like It, V. I)

We have blind spots, limitations, and weaknesses and there is little you can do about it alone other than live life in real, caring and truthful community with others you give permission to speak into your life.

Our limitations and weaknesses are every bit as true about us as the things that are wonderful and to ignore them is to enter the next season of life with only half of a whole picture. If your next season of life is less about what you do and more about living out of the real, true you, then you need to accommodate all of you, even if it hurts.

There is good news even in your limitations. In the chapter 'Unique Personality' we examine how your unique personality type is abundant in strengths but like a coin, it is two-sided. Your strengths have corresponding weaknesses. This is inevitable. It is ok. Or to put it a better way, your weaknesses and limitations have corresponding strengths. Your greatest liability can be your greatest strength in the right context.

Friends tell me I am quite sensitive, and in business have often undervalued my role because I wanted to place the relationships at the centre. This can cause inequality and problems in the world of business and it is called 'people pleasing'. But, valuing people and being sensitive to the needs of others is a strength in the right context. We may not be able to change our nature but we can ensure we plant ourselves in the right landscape.

We must have the courage to turn around and look at the landscape of our life and be honest about what has not happened for us. We must identify which limitations exist both internal, and around us.

To give you an example, my internal frontiers included my sensitive nature, (perhaps over-sensitive), that I can be impatient and get bored quickly (due to being quite creative), and I am probably quite idealistic which can create exaggerated feelings of disappointment. External limitations included that we have three sons in school so moving to a new inspirational job in Botswana, or wherever, was not going to be workable. I also noted that getting a full-time job would be tricky because I had been self-employed as an entrepreneur for so long I would be a nightmare to manage (seven years breaking rules not following them.) Since selling my business, I had made commitments to various charities, individuals, and had a deep desire to enable my wife Hazel to follow her vocation. This meant it would be hard to honour those commitments if I were in an office somewhere forty five hours a week forty-eight weeks a year. The list went on and on.

What are your weaknesses and limitations?

1. List them.
2. If you are brave ask two or three people you know and trust who have seen you in different contexts over the last twenty years and ask them to write a list.
3. Next to each weakness write down how it could potentially become a strength.

Unique Personality

"Sooner or later we must distinguish between what we are not and what we are".

Ian Morgan Cron

So far this book has explored digging deeper into yourself rather than looking outside. It is about 'peeling the onion' so to speak. If you are to find a vocation and cause to live for, then knowing how you are wired and what makes you 'tick' is all important.

We have already established that you have unique gifts, (things you appear to have been born naturally good at). You have unique passions (things that make your heart sing or scream and when talking about them you sit more upright and there is a certain sparkle about you). You have unique skills, (things you have become accomplished at as a result of learning/nurture). We also explored limitations and weaknesses and how they can be such a true guide because on the flip side of each weakness there is probably a veiled strength.

This chapter is all about your unique personality.

It is a strange thing that our true personality can be hidden from view. Who are you when no one else is looking and when you feel no pressure to behave in a certain way? Our true personalities become hidden and yes, even distorted over the years for many reasons.

There are several reputable tools used by Human Resource professionals and counsellors to help people better understand their personalities. The essence of these theories is that much random variation in behaviour is actually quite orderly and consistent. Myers Briggs is a well-known tool you can use, and it identifies sixteen different distinct personality types based on:

- A. Whether you are an extrovert or introvert, (prefer to focus on the inner or outer world);
- B. How you process information, (sensing or intuition);
- C. How you make decisions, (based on logic or feelings);
- D. Your approach to structure and whether you need clear decisions or whether you are open to remaining open to new ideas, (judging vs perceiving).

Myers Briggs is a helpful tool but the one I have found to be even more helpful and dynamic is the Enneagram. You can read more at the Enneagram Institute.

We all have a basic personality type and the reason this is of such fundamental importance is because:

I. People do not change from one personality type to another.
II. Different cultures favour and reward some personality types over others so unless you are clear on your own, the chance is you will morph into what your culture tells you it wants you to be rather than your true self.

In his book 'The Road Back to You: An Enneagram Journey to Self-Discovery' Ian Morgan Cron writes,

"Human beings are wired for survival. As little kids we instinctually place a mask called personality over parts of our authentic self to protect us from harm and make our way in the world. Made up of innate qualities, coping strategies, conditioned reflexes and defense mechanisms, among lots of other things, our personality helps us know and do what we sense is required to please our parents, to fit in and relate well to our friends, to satisfy the expectations of our culture and to get our basic needs met."

And,

"Sooner or later we must distinguish between what we are not and what we are. We must accept the fact that we are not what we would like to be. We must cast off our false, exterior self like the cheap and showy garment that it is"

Helpful thoughts I am sure you agree. I think I re-read those paragraphs about five times. You may need to take time out to make a cup of tea and think about this before reading any further. The implications are far-reaching.

By all means, ask your two-three close friends but know that they will only be able to say what they see and maybe they cannot see your true hidden nature. Maybe you behave like an extrovert and are an 'up front' sort of person because those are the people who get the promotions at work, but in fact, you are more of an introvert and spend much of your time exhausted. Maybe you have believed the lie that only loud visible leaders are valuable. My headmaster at school once said to us:

"Gentlemen, in this world there are leaders and there are followers, it's your choice".

'Choice' is an interesting word. It sounded more like as young men we were being asked to choose between being lions or lambs. Between victors and victims. Success or failure. Which would you pick? Maybe you have your own stories about times when you subtly steered away from who you were in favour of who you ought to be in an attempt to conform and gain approval from those in authority over you.

I will briefly take you through the nine distinct basic personality types that exist within the Enneagram theory, (www.enneagraminstitute.com). I am sure one or two of them will resonate, but take a free online Enneagram test and read around the subject.

Type One – The Perfectionist.

At your best you serve others with integrity and are patient with the process and details in achieving excellence. But at your worst you will fixate on small imperfections in things and even other people and may be controlling. This is because you feel a burden to fix the world around you and do not see errors as inevitable. Famous Perfectionist: Nelson Mandela

Type Two - The Helper

At your best you are warm, generous and other people focused and want others to be happy. You want to help people flourish. You see their needs and rush to be the answer. You are probably drawn to influential people. On a bad day, you will probably lack proper boundaries and allow your own needs to go unmet, and do things with the expectation of emotional payback such as respect, appreciation or a stronger friendship. Famous Helper: Princess Diana

Type Three – The Performer

Performers are high achievers and are gifted and committed to doing things well. Normally lots of things simultaneously. You are probably known for taking on far more than other people and doing those things well. But, on a bad day a performers identity becomes tied to what they have achieved because they believe they "are what they do" and they find failure unacceptable so are hard on themselves and also on others.   Famous Performer: Tiger Woods

Type four – The Romantic

Romantics have broad emotional ranges and are attuned to creativity, beauty and connectedness. There is a desire for people to see them as unique and on a bad day romantics can be melodramatic in the desire to be seen. They also compare themselves with others which can be a vice. Famous Romantic: Vincent Van Gogh

Type five – The Investigator

Investigators like to observe situations and be led by their thoughts more than their feelings. They have an in-depth knowledge about many things and like to share that knowledge. On a bad day, they find it hard to depend on others, are defensive and cut themselves off from others. Famous Investigator: Bill Gates

Type Six – The Loyalist

Loyalists hope for the best but prepare for the worst. They have a strong need for security and support. On the healthy side, loyalists plan and think through things logically but often from a risk management point of view and with one eye on what can go wrong in most situations. Loyalists are loyal to their core friends and beliefs and are excellent at troubleshooting but on a bad day overthink, and over worry and are fearful, and sceptical.   Famous Loyalist: Ben Stiller

Type Seven – The Enthusiast

Enthusiasts are extroverted, optimistic, and spontaneous. They have a zest for life and they are often the life and soul of a party. They enjoy adventures, last-minute ideas and seek happiness. But, on a bad day enthusiasts avoid responsibilities where it may prove painful and may find it easier to start things than finish them. They look for the positive in everything which can create a disconnect with reality. Famous Enthusiast: Elton John

Type 8 - The Challenger

Challengers are strong, commanding leaders who are passionate and people like to follow them. On a bad day however, a 'Challenger' can be dualistic in their thinking and struggle to accommodate opposing views, or embrace ambiguity. This means their passion and convictions whilst a strength can come across as 'pushy'. Famous Challenger: Winston Churchill.

Type 9 – The Peacemaker

Peacemakers are natural mediators, accepting and trustworthy. They can hold different views together and bring people together. The flip side of this harmonious strength is that they seldom rock the boat and therefore do not consider their own needs which can cause self-neglect or resentment.

Famous Peacemaker: The Queen. Elizabeth the Second, by the Grace of God of the United Kingdom of Great Britain and Northern Ireland and of Her other Realms and Territories Queen, Head of the Commonwealth, Defender of the Faith.

Please do a full test online and read all about your basic personality type(s). Whilst we are formed throughout our life, our basic personality type will probably mirror the way we were as a child.

I have already used the phrase 'against the grain of your soul' in this book. The idea is that there are things that 'fit' with who you are and there are therefore things that do not 'fit'. If you go against the grain of your true self, you will get 'splinters'. I already stated that one cannot change their personality type and if that is true then you need to make sure you fit your context and environment with your personality. Plants that flourish in thirty degrees centigrade and an arid climate are unlikely to survive in Greenland and the reverse is also true.

Self-disclosure: My Enneagram type is that of a Helper. All the short statements you read about that personality type are unbelievably true of me. I love being the answer to other people's problems and offering support directly or indirectly. I draw identity and self-worth out if it. The reward is simply knowing I have helped someone whether that help is advice or digging a hole. For me there is ample meaning and purpose in that and it feels especially healthy when there is an element of sacrifice or inconvenience on my part in helping.

However, on a bad day, my desire to 'help' is not as unconditional as it should be and that is unhealthy. It turns out that when I am tired or 'down' the absence of respect or gratitude from the intended recipient creates anxiety followed by mild anger and annoyance. It is the negative feeling of being used and taken advantage of even though I volunteered myself into the 'helping'. It is quite a conundrum. I quite literally 'ask for it'.

This goes to show that our strengths and weaknesses are two sides of the same coin and therefore inevitable. The resulting tensions need to be managed rather than altogether eliminated.

Knowing your personality type is a helpful guide for what you do in your life. If you are an introvert, finding a vocation that involves a constant human interaction will probably be exhausting for you. If you are an Enthusiast, you will probably not flourish in an environment which requires a systematic, long-term approach built around small but important details. If you are a loyalist, you might struggle to offer inspirational team leadership in a context where you cannot see the way ahead. (Leaders always have to offer that even if it means digging very deep indeed).

There are exceptions to the norms I describe. In fact, in a recent conversation with a friend, he shared how one of his high points in life was during his early twenties when he spoke in school assemblies on a daily basis even though he was and still is, fairly introvert. Part of the satisfaction came from rising to the challenge and doing things that felt beyond him. I accept that. However, I would question whether that would have been a sustainable way of life over twenty years or whether he would have depleted his energies sooner rather than later.

The key message I am sharing is not a complex one: You are uniquely shaped, designed and gifted on every level including your personality, and the best way to honour your unique 'make-up' where possible, is to align what you 'do' with who you 'are' inside.

It is a bit like cutlery. A spoon is perfectly crafted for eating soup. Have you ever attempted that with a fork? Similarly, a serrated knife is perfectly designed for cutting a steak. Have you ever attempted that task with a spoon? They have different functions and so do we.

Don Riso writes,

"Every moment has the possibility of delighting us, nurturing us, supporting us - if we are here to see it. Life is a tremendous gift, but most of us are missing it because we are watching a mental movie of our lives instead. As we learn to trust in the moment and to value awareness, we learn how to turn off the internal mood projector and start living a much more interesting life - the one we are actually starring in."

Do you look at yourself through a lens that blurs your personality? The best gift, the most long-lasting legacy, the most colourful expression, and the most purposeful and meaningful contribution you can give to the world and those you love is to be unequivocally and unashamedly yourself.

Uniquely Motivated

"Show me the incentive and I will show you the outcome".

Charlie Munger

What motivates and inspires you to do things? Imagine a steam train: There is a cast iron vehicle, train tracks lining the way to a destination, perhaps an ornate hardwood interior and a cylinder and piston linked to the coal-fired steam boiler? It is all magnificent but useless without fire. What is the fire that will make movement possible in your onward journey after reading these chapters?

Motivation: a reason or reasons for acting or behaving in a particular way. Synonyms include stimulus and inspiration.

In England, we sometimes describe motivation as 'oomph', and we will all too often hear people say 'I can't be bothered.' We are all wired differently and there will be different things that drive us. Doing anything vaguely worthwhile requires huge amounts of energy and a certain fire in one's belly.

In the chapters on Gifts and Passions, I described passion as the thing that makes you sparkle, sit upright, and become animated. That is a real clue to what motivates you but motivation takes you one step further and provides the 'why' behind you taking the decision to act. Not the why you WANT to take action but the why you DO take action. It is the bridge that connects your passion to your subsequent steps. Many people in life day dream and think noble thoughts about building a better world, but only a handful have the motivation to act.

Motivation is a moving target. That is to say, not only are the sources of motivation (which I will go into, shortly) broad in scope but also they change in each season of life. For some, there is a desire to make money plain and simple. In fact, I have known people who grew up in relative poverty and were driven in adult life to make sure they never went to that place again with a strong instinct to insulate their own kin from that predicament. Other people are propelled by vanity and perhaps ego. To them money equals a Porsche 911 or a Business Class plane ticket. Underlying this extravagance may be a love of cars and/or aviation but perhaps the real reason for such luxuries is that they feed into a feeling of self-worth.

Anger motivates some people and they have a desire to change the world because they are angry at a particular injustice and finding a solution to that issue occupies their waking thoughts. Many are motivated to action by a desire for legacy after living many decades curving inwards, they come to the revelation it did not satisfy their craving for significance, or scratch the itch for a purpose and they do something utterly altruistic so that they can have dignity and leave something beautiful after them.

It is a true place of wholeness which all men and women can come to that their deepest real identity need not be in what they do at all but in their intrinsic worth and value as loved human beings which is not tied to the 'ups' and the 'downs' of life but in an idea called Grace. On this subject I recommend my wife's favourite book called 'The Ragamuffin Gospel' by Brennan Manning.

When I first engaged in selling my company (the one that sought to help people find the right legal advice and provide free legal guidance and information), a complicated process inviting interested parties to sign non-disclosure agreements and then make offers, took place. One of the interested parties was not a private equity company but rather an entrepreneur like me and after a two hour conversation he told me he saw himself in me. He said:

"You've been told you are not the sort of person who can build a business and you want to prove everyone wrong don't you?."

It was in fact a revelation to me that I was motivated in part from that deep place. A school teacher once told me I was not a 'high flyer' and should stay away from law altogether. It was like telling a child not to press a red button. It caused a deep wound in me because it made me feel I was not good enough and my first business was to prove her wrong. It had as much to do with that emotional transaction as it had with running a business. It was like someone who suffers from vertigo doing a bungee jump. Facing fears, living dreams and all of that. How complex and fascinating we all are. I share this to make a simple but profound point that we have steel inside of us, and a fire from within if we can only locate it. It may come from an unexpected place.

Motivation can be intrinsic/internal such as a feeling of contentment, satisfaction, joy and fulfilment from a job well done. Conversely, motivation can be extrinsic such as a financial bonus, a pay rise, or the fear of being fired. This explains why people who could earn a fortune at Goldman Sachs end up working as teachers in inner-city schools or as pastors and community organisers in urban priority areas. Conversely, it is why some people seem willing to work twenty four seven (sell their soul) for a company with a product that does not really matter in the scheme of things.

In this chapter I want to stimulate some thought about what motivates you today and what has motivated you in the past. Hopefully, this will help you find new fire to fuel serious action in the months and years ahead. You will need it.

Motivated by Incentive

This is the one that underpins much of the free market economy. The famous industrialist, lawyer, architect and value investor Charlie Munger once said

"Show me the incentive and I will show you the outcome".

As a rule of thumb, people act out of self-interest and align their behaviour with what makes most sense for them individually. There is a famous Federal Express business case study involving a logistics problem they could not overcome. Their unique selling point was overnight delivery and any delay that hindered that killed their entire business model. They brought in many top managers to explore how they could better unload and re-load planes and so speed up the turnaround. The work involved new training, better machinery and higher hourly pay. None of these initiatives worked.

Eventually (as I understand it) a shrewd manager changed the way they paid people from per hour to per 'turn around' meaning unload one plane and re-load. This was the epicentre of their logistics problem. Suddenly, it meant that workers got paid the same whether they took six hours or three hours. They realised they could double their effective wage by getting the job done more quickly and as you can imagine the front-line workers themselves solved this problem and within the week, the planes were being unloaded and re-loaded in the required timescale. Problem solved.

Incentives are powerful and shape human behaviour. It is not all bad as perhaps that financial reward will enable you to do great things down the track. Also, it is perfectly possible to be motivated by both financial incentives and the goal of achievement.

Motivated by the need to achieve

People are commonly motivated by the desire to achieve a goal and/or accomplish a task. People climb Mount Everest for various reasons other than the wonderful view. The main one being the sense of achievement. In the first half of life people want to 'prove' themselves and earn the respect of their peers and those they respect through what they achieve in sport, business and life. If achievement creates a fire in your belly, you are probably self-motivated and process orientated and love the thought of the challenge and the process of accomplishment as much as the end goal.

Motivated through fear and failure

This is a negative motivator. Many entrepreneurs I have met came from humble beginnings and relative poverty. It was this early experience that formed their sense of aspiration and true grit. Fears can take many forms. I recall having a real drive to make my first start-up work because I felt claustrophobic as part of a law firm where I had to account for every six minutes of my day. It was a real fear of being trapped and not being free to be myself. I was also fearful of being unable to be a present Dad and having my diary in the hands of people who did not know my name. In other words I was in a way running from something as opposed to running to something.

One of my heroes is the Scottish tennis player Andy Murray. He was clearly motivated by a fear of losing. In his own words, not dissimilar to those echoed by many elite athletes:

'We had to take a long hard look [at ourselves and] ... we were disappointed that we didn't perform, but that was a massive learning curve.'

'It was the kick up the backside [that we needed] ... so it made us work that extra bit harder over the next two months.'

Motivated by power

This sounds awfully cold hearted and it can be. If you have watched the Netflix series House of Cards you will consider this to be a dark motivating force due to the risk of Machiavelli like behaviour where the end justifies the means. The desire for power also reminds me of 'The Lord of The Rings' and how everyone wanted the ring of power. In fact, the only one who could carry it was the one who did not want it (Frodo). Tolkien was a true philosopher.

To quote Lord Acton, a British historian of the late 19th century

"Power tends to corrupt; absolute power corrupts absolutely".

But, there is a brighter side to power. There is a legitimate desire for power to influence and shape lives for the better. Sometimes power is the only way to bring about change. I believe Nelson Mandela desired political power to right the wrongs wrought on South African Society by Apartheid. He had twenty-seven years imprisoned on Robin Island to think about such things and his time in office was transformational for that nation and a model of reconciliation for onlookers everywhere. Would that have been possible without having political power?

I have friends who have sought influence at a city level in Bristol in order to address social ills such as food poverty, homelessness, illiteracy, and supporting the rehabilitation of offenders. Power and influence can be noble motivators; it all depends on what is in one's heart.

Motivated by social and community connections

Humans are innately communal ,or tribal, and have the desire to connect with others. Some say this is the reason Facebook grew from nothing to 2.6 billion connected people in under fifteen years. Facebook enabled people to eloquently organise themselves into groups and communicate with less friction than previous generations could.

Social connections can satisfy a desire to serve the wider world and nurture the place of our family and friends within it. I have seen this motivation show itself in people who are born networkers and they gain satisfaction and reward from being a 'point' person and having the respect of those served by that community. This is a place of honour and for many it 'itches a scratch' to help others. Referring back to the Enneagram theories surrounding personality types, I suspect 'Helpers - Personality type two are probably motivated by these sorts of activities.

Motivated by learning and growing in competence

Some people are motivated by their internal need and desire to learn and better themselves. Such people may be avid readers, especially reading books which enable them to learn from other people they respect. In fact, such people may undertake impossible undesirable tasks because they relish what they may learn as a result.

There may be many other motivations in addition to those mentioned above. The key thing to note is that we all get out of bed in the morning for different reasons and there is nothing wrong in this. But, in your own quest for vocation, meaning and fruitfulness you must recognise the fire you have in your belly.

If you have no fire that is a problem. Without fire there is no heat, without heat there can be no steam, and no steam means the pistons will not turn and there will be no movement for the train referred to back in the first paragraph. Without action dreams remain just that....*dreams*.

What do I do if I have no motivation?

The problem with self-help books (and this does not claim to be one), is that they often suggest you do something simple which is not rocket science but beyond your grasp. Let me give you an example. When we lose something, how often do people ask: "Where did you last see it"? If we knew that it would not be lost would it?

This entire book is exploring change. Change of vocation, values and motivations. The things that once motivated you may no longer do the trick. Aged twenty-three, in a serious relationship and wanting to buy a house, financial incentive was a strong motivation. It was not the motivation of money, but the motivation of achieving the goal of owning a house in which I could start a family. Fast forward fifteen years and the goals and motivations are quite different.

It could be that today you are not motivated by money, achievement, power, social recognition or even failure. In fact you feel wholly unmotivated and lacking any fire in your belly at all. What should you do? Do not despair or be hard on yourself as it is a common predicament and one that can be overcome.

The first thing to do is re-discover your passion. At this point you may wish to re-read that chapter 'Uniquely Passionate'. What are your goals and dreams? Re-evaluate what they are and whether they still matter to you. If your goals and the tasks linked to them do not energise you, then a lack of motivation is inevitable. This is easier said than done because it is not outwardly visible or obvious but emanates from the core of your being. This is why a journey of self-discovery is so important. Where you find the treasure of your own passion, I suspect you will find hidden in plain sight the treasure of motivation.

I have heard it said,

"Where the head leads the heart follows".

This is helpful. It is the idea that many important aspects of our life (marriage, friendships, public service) do not need to be mastered by feelings. Feelings are fickle and like the British weather can change five times in a day. Rather, in all sorts of situations we sometimes start with duty which can express itself in disciplines, which can grow into dedication and then that grows into desire or even fascination. In this book, the author hopes that the rational and objective questions around your inner 'wiring' will provide some direction and then the motivation and passion can grow as you go.

Unique Coordinates

I hope you have enjoyed reading thus far. I have tried to be transparent about the fact that this is not a book of answers but rather a book of questions. It asks the overriding question 'How do I go about answering the question: what should I do with the rest of my life?" If you already have some clarity please keep asking the same questions because you will find the answers ferment like wine over time and can be quite nuanced.

Before navigating begins you need to put yourself on the map. I hope the questions asked earlier in this book can help you to do that. As a recap so far we have asked:

A. What are your gifts? What are you good at? What do you just 'get' to the extent that it is effortless, autonomous and seems like you can do it without even thinking?

B. What are your passions? What makes your soul sing? When are you animated, energised and in a zone where time passes quickly?

C. What are your weaknesses and limitations? What things, internal and external shape your reality?

D. What is your basic personality type? You cannot change it, so ignoring this reality will cause long term friction.

E. What motivates you? What factors turn your thoughts into action? Your motivations will change in different seasons of life but what motivates you right now?

If your future direction could be laid out on a map, then each of these questions provide coordinates for you to use. By including them in your vision for the future, they will together provide you with a clear direction.

They may not tell you what to do but I hope that they will together form a filter through which you run your plans and ideas to ensure that they align with who you really are. One thing is clear, whatever you do, wherever you go, YOU will be there. You are the common denominator in your future course and therefore it simply needs to accommodate the true version of who you really are.

The chapters that follow are exciting. They will take you to the edge of your comfort zone and nudge you to 'go for it'. They will include preparing you for change and helping you understand how change happens in real life. Then you will begin to define a personal vision, and followed by some personal research and development before taking firm steps.

But, each of the steps in the paragraph above need to be consistent with the things you have learned about yourself so far or you risk replacing one mask with another and becoming another best version of someone else and not you. That would be such a shame for the world around you.

'Truths about me' statements

We will now turn your answers and reflections into short paragraphs which should embody some clear truthful statements that you must reference going forward, (unless you need to change any answers). By truthful we simply mean that they frame your current reality. These statements are not intended to be carved into stone and thereby label and characterise you forever more, rather they are meant to function as a filter or triage in the way you assess things going forward.

I am naturally good at < feel free to name a couple of things or write a short sentence that explains it>,

I feel energised, engaged and in my zone when I am < name a couple of activities or describe what you are passionate about>.

Through experience and education I have become quite skilled at <do not recite your LinkedIn profile, just name the skills which stand out, or that has defined your work to date>.

I have both weaknesses and limitations and the main ones which seem to have impacted me and those around me are <name a couple of internal weaknesses, or external realities which impact you whether you like it or not>.

My basic personality type is < Name your Enneagram type(s). You will have needed to take the free online test to do this> **and the main characteristics of my personality are,** < name the two to three key things that are true of your personality make up>.

The things that most motivate me right now are <name a couple of things, money, justice, fear, building community connections>

Now, read it out to yourself as many times as you feel comfortable. Does it resonate?

If it does you are in the minority. For me it did not at first and that is because we have become so accustomed to being a less than the true and crisp version of ourselves for a myriad of reasons already discussed. The truth of what makes us tick and how we are designed is true even if we do not feel it at first. That is why it is so valuable to dig deep for answers and to ask important questions and then let the answers grow on you.

We knew of a family who spent many months sailing around the world with young children. They learned to walk at sea. On their return home the children struggled to walk on dry land and were off balance because they had become so adept at balancing on deck and had developed 'sea legs'. It took a few weeks to recover their more natural 'land legs'. The same may be true of how you feel about your truth statements. Give them some time.

What do you do if the answers feel foreign?

1. Do the exercise as many times as you need and feel free to change your answers as long as they are truthful about you. This is not intended to be easy, it is intended to be helpful.
2. Submit your 'Truth about Me' statements to your inner circle of friends who know you best and go through them one by one. There are some major life questions which justify asking the same question four hundred times until you have clarity.

This book is in no way meant to be autobiographical as that would wholly undermine the premise that we are all very unique. The personal challenge I experienced though was in not seeing how the various truth statements could fit together later in a 'job description' or outcome. I was focussed on the questions but I would be lying if I did not admit that at every stage of this journey of self-discovery, I had one eye on what the answer would eventually be in terms of how I should actually pivot and what I should do.

It felt a bit like a murder mystery film where I was the detective picking up clues along the way constantly looking for an ultimate answer in the end of 'who' or 'what'? For you that may be clear but perhaps the end game is not an outcome or product but rather a new way of seeing things: Life is not a factory to turn you into something despite what education establishments might sometimes have you believe.

My own (slightly edited) truth statements look like this:

I am naturally good at forming new ideas, spotting opportunities and trends early on and caring for people.

I feel energised, engaged and in my zone when I am imagining new things that do not yet exist and explaining the possibilities to others and how an idea could be transformed to a reality.

Through work and education I have become quite skilled at being rational in decision making, understanding other people and giving helpful advice.

My weaknesses include being quite shy and reluctant to be in leadership. I can be quite sensitive. **My limitations include** that we are quite tied to one geographical area due to the children's education.

My basic personality type is a Helper **and the main characteristics of my personality are,** that I value relationships highly and am able to empathise with the needs of others.

The things that most motivate me right now are wanting to do something that significantly impacts the world for the better.

How do these 'truths about me' statements help? I run possibilities through them like they are a water filter. Let me give you an example: In exploring my own next season of life, the opportunity arose to apply for the role of Chief Executive Officer for an international charity. It had been in existence for over thirty years and was established and needed solid leadership and stability.

Using my filter I was able to ask more of the right questions. Will this role allow me to predominantly create new ideas, dream and spend time with people? Probably not. Would this role allow me to enter my own zone of creativity, imagination and communication? Probably not. Could I make rational people-centric decisions? Probably yes. Would my weakness of avoiding leadership and being quite sensitive, lend itself to being in such a role? Not a reason to say no but yes there would be friction. What about my personality type of predominantly helping and empathising with people? My gut told me it would mostly involve me making 'greater good' decisions based on spreadsheets. And finally, what about my motivation to make the world a better place and feel like I have made a contribution to the world my kid's will grow up in? Almost certainly a yes. So, as you can see my 'truth statements' gave a mediocre thumbs up but not enough to apply for the role because I knew I needed to be expressing creativity in the form of problem solving ideas that help people.

A further opportunity arose to join a legal start up business which I had originally been instrumental in founding, (my idea, branding, initiation etc), but I subsequently stepped back to allow the other founders room to take the helm. The question was, did I want to become the Chief Executive Officer? Using my filter, was so helpful. Could I form new ideas, and be creative in strategy and gathering a team of like-minded people? Almost certainly yes. Could I be passionate about their business plan? Maybe, if it had a social element. Would my perceived weaknesses be problematic? Maybe. As for my motivations I do not think there is a fit as the main driver for the team would be financial incentive whereas for me it would be social impact. So, armed with these truths I was able to decline the invitation but offer to be helpful as a friend.

On the next page there is a simple diagram illustrating how your unique truth statements might function as a filter for any new ideas or opportunities which arise. Put simply you look at new opportunities through the lens of your unique qualities and then give the new opportunity a score.

In exploring your life pivot, I hope that you too can use this as a tool to help you weigh-up and score the possibilities and ensure that whatever you do is in harmony with the grain of your true and unique self.

It is not about idealism but thinking things through carefully. It is a bit like road markings, these statements will not get you to your destination but they can ensure you do not end up off the road and in a ditch.

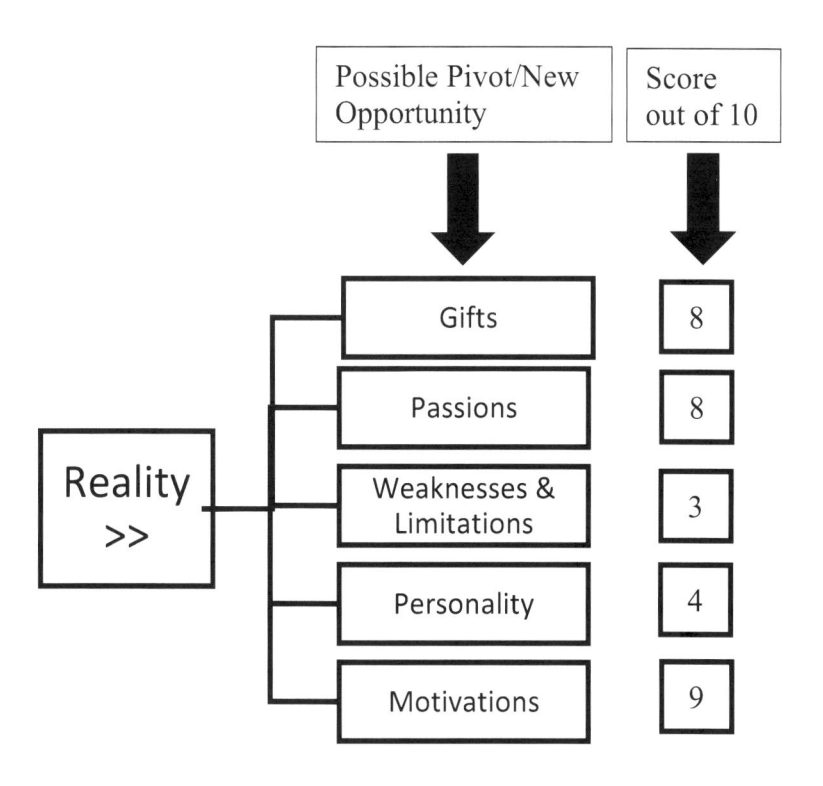

```
                            ┌─────────────────────┐    ┌──────────┐
                            │ Possible Pivot/New  │    │  Score   │
                            │ Opportunity         │    │ out of 10│
                            └──────────┬──────────┘    └────┬─────┘
                                       ▼                    ▼
                                  ┌─────────┐           ┌──────┐
                                  │  Gifts  │           │  8   │
                                  └─────────┘           └──────┘
                                  ┌─────────┐           ┌──────┐
                                  │ Passions│           │  8   │
                                  └─────────┘           └──────┘
              ┌──────────┐        ┌───────────────┐     ┌──────┐
              │ Reality  │────────│ Weaknesses &  │     │  3   │
              │   >>     │        │ Limitations   │     └──────┘
              └──────────┘        └───────────────┘
                                  ┌─────────────┐       ┌──────┐
                                  │ Personality │       │  4   │
                                  └─────────────┘       └──────┘
                                  ┌─────────────┐       ┌──────┐
                                  │ Motivations │       │  9   │
                                  └─────────────┘       └──────┘
```

Process of change

"We are what we repeatedly do. Excellence then is not an act, but a habit."
Aristotle

We are forever changing from one thing to another. It is just a case of from what and into what? When we talk about finding a cause and passion to live for, change will be at the heart of that process because the assumption is that right now you are not engaged in something that makes your heart sing. If you are, stop reading and please mentor some other people.

We dislike change as a species but it is inevitable. The houses we live in, the friends we keep, our places of employment, hobbies, country of residence and even whether you prefer a latte or flat white. We are habit forming creatures.

If you are to stand any chance of aligning how you pour out your life with your true gifts, passions and skills, weaknesses, personality and motivations then you will need to change a few things. Perhaps the first change will be to your vision. How do you imagine your future?

In this chapter, I explore how change happens and the three things that make up the tripod of transformation.

Transformation happens because of three things.

i. What we believe;
ii. What we do, (habits);
iii. The people we spend time with.

To transition from one season to another you will need to change on many levels but I specifically want to share some simple ideas which I found to be enormously helpful.

A. The people you spend time with.

You may have heard it said you are the average of the five people you spend most of your time with. Are you deliberate and intentional about who you have in the inner circle of your life? Over time, the process of osmosis means your thoughts, values, behaviour patterns, and therefore your actions, habits, character and thereafter your destiny are influenced and shaped by the people in your life.

This is not some mystical process; you will notice that in certain groups the conversation will often gravitate in a particular direction. There may be attitudes which invoke social responsibility and aspirational dreams to shape the world around you. Whereas in other social groups there may be aspirations to have a wine cooler in the kitchen and a Tesla in the driveway. Not that these things are evil in themselves but rather we eventually reflect what we focus on. We walk down the road we stare down. Do you agree? It is often referred to as peer pressure. We have tribal instincts to conform to those around us.

I am not for one minute advocating a solitary utopia in which you only let people near to you who make you happy. In life, we meet so many people who find life difficult and it is noble and necessary that we all curve outwards to care for others. I am talking about your inner circle. Those you most confide in.

Each year my wife and I have a strategy day and we look at almost every area of life to discuss and agree on our priorities. "What will define us this year?" It is a wonderful way to spend a day and recognize we have the gift of choice. It is within your power to do certain things and say 'no' to others. We discuss our finances, hobbies, work, family time, giving, and one of the most important for us is friendships.

We draw three concentric circles on a big sheet of A3 (like an archery target) and the inner circle is the 'bull's eye', and that is reserved for up to three people we each trust the most who we give a virtual 'backstage pass' to our hearts and lives, our fears, and dreams. It takes much trust built up over many years (decades) to share on that level. Then there is the second group and that is for people who we care about greatly and share almost everything. Then there is the larger group in which we find at least eighty percent of our friends. I think even without this image, we all have something similar.

For this chapter, I would encourage you to do the exercise yourself and draw the three circles and write who in your life inhabits each circle. Those closest to you will shape and influence you.

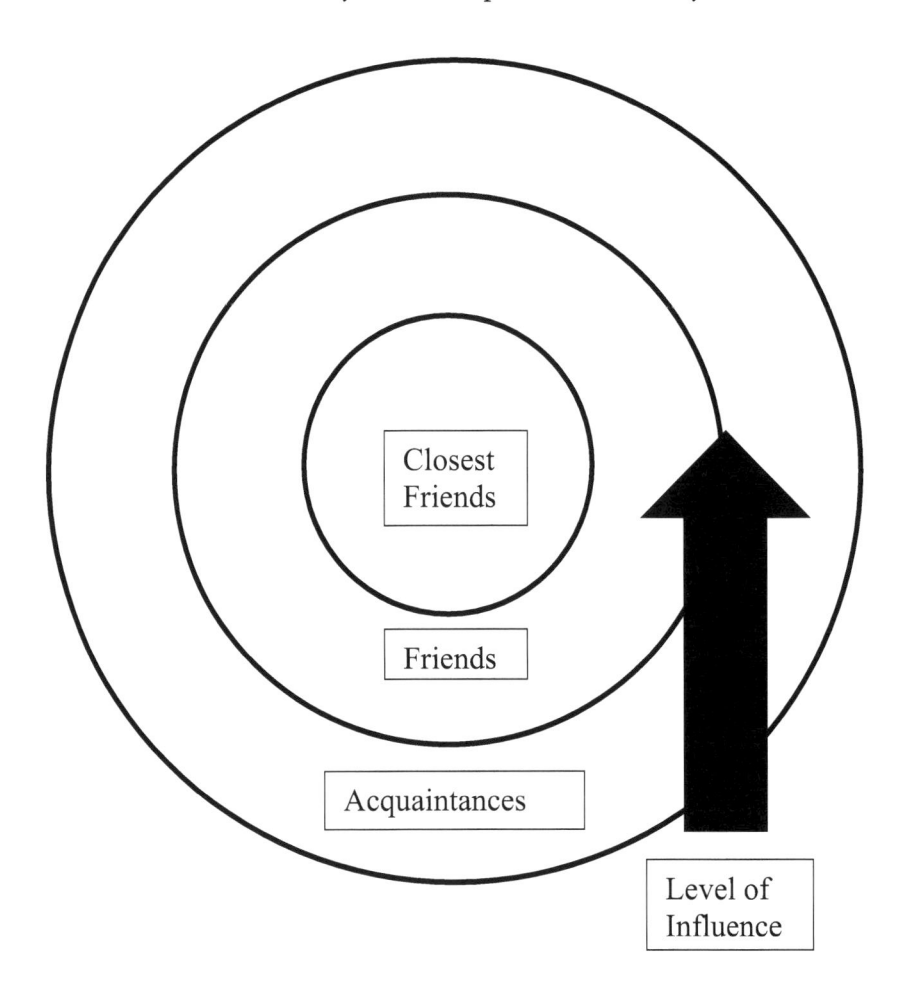

In my early career, I practiced as a lawyer in the UK and I recall drafting schedules of special damages for serious personal injury claims where the people would never work again. There was an authority called the 'Ogden' tables which provided formulas with various multipliers for future loss of earnings. For children with no earnings history, their future losses were based on how much their parents earned. What a depressing thought. It was there in black and white that the highest Courts in the land upheld the cynical idea that an apple rarely fell far from the tree. Fortunately, with mentors, conviction, and passion this pattern can be overcome. The simple point I want to make is that you must be acutely aware that those around you…shape you.

On the plus side, this principle works in reverse and it is exciting that we will replicate what we celebrate and be what we can see. Our conversations will impact the way we think and what we think will eventually impact our behaviour. We can use this law of nature to propel ourselves into our unique and passionate vocation but we must ensure that our inner circle of friends and influencers include people who are for us, not against us, and committed to our journey of becoming the best version of ourselves and not someone else.

I have read many articles on picking the best friends. It all sounds a little inward looking and narcissistic. However, you need friends who are wise, who share your values, vision and purpose. They need to see who you could become rather than just who you have been. They need to challenge you and hold you to account on who you are becoming. I love the Proverb of Solomon that says:

"Wounds from a friend can be trusted, but an enemy multiplies kisses".

Are your closest friends 'yes' people who will always just cheer you on, or are you fortunate to have friends who care enough for you to be truthful? If so, you have hit the jackpot. Such friends are rare.

B. Shaped through our habits

A few words from some famous philosophers:

"We are what we repeatedly do. Excellence then is not an act, but a habit." – Aristotle

"Men's natures are alike; it is their habits that separate them." – Confucius

Every day we wake up and there are things that define us. Our habits. There are things we habitually do and they help or hinder who we are becoming and what we are able or unable to do. Athletes will know this to be true more than the rest of us.

Certain habits will come to mind right away for you. They will include addictions, such as staring at a screen but also the time you wake up and go to sleep and the things you eat and drink. Habits will include the hobbies that entertain you in your free time. You have heard it said 'you are what you eat'? That is true, over a six-month period every cell in your body is replaced and constructed entirely of what enters your body in the form of nutrition or otherwise. The same is true of your soul and mind.

If you 'Google' healthy habits you will find 132,000,000 pages on the subject. They will suggest you have a prescribed bedtime and wake up time, daily exercise, limited alcohol, and a structured diet. These may all prove to be helpful but I would like to share my take on a handful of habits which I have found to be invaluable.

There are many helpful habits that could be mentioned but the ones I would like to mention have in common the single goal of quietening our minds, and removing unnecessary distractions so that we can be more reflective than the twenty-first century normally allows.

Habit One – Keep a journal

Journals may sound like something only Earnest Shackleton, the explorer might keep but you should keep one too. I have kept a journal on and off over the years and I have found that when I do, I am more reflective, deliberate and intentional. I am more aware of my own feelings and moods. I find I suddenly notice the frictions more, and also the things that are life-giving. I end up pondering more frequently, 'why did I say yes to that?"

I heard a quote last week by business writer Jim Collins which was so helpful. He said:

"The greatest danger is not failure, the greatest danger is to be successful without understanding why you were successful in the first place."

I like this quote because it is so positive. It seems that we so often put our failures down to our personal deficiencies and our 'wins' down to luck. This is not true. When things have gone well, and you were there, then just maybe you have inadvertently stumbled upon the intersection between your unique capabilities, passions and personality. Carving out time to reflect is essential if you are to notice these moments so that you can do more of them.

Journals make fascinating reading after the event but the main reason I find it to be an essential habit is that it makes you pay more attention on the journey. This is especially important if you are to see the 'secrets hidden in plain sight' in your life (referred to in other chapters). Journals are a wonderful tool to help you pay attention to your own life and live in the present.

Habit two - Choose simplicity

Steve Jobs is famous for the iPhone which has created (ironically) one of the biggest enemies to simplicity. In fact, the average adult touches their iPhone 2500 times a day. But he said:

"Simple can be harder than complex" "That's been one of my mantras — focus and simplicity. Simple can be harder than complex: You have to work hard to get your thinking clean to make it simple. But it's worth it in the end because once you get there, you can move mountains." ~Steve Jobs~

Life is busy. Being busy apparently equals being important.

Almost every chapter of this book requires you to go away and put the kettle on, have a cup of tea, and sit in a quiet room. These are big questions with serious implications for your life and those you love. It is about becoming the very best and most true version of yourself.

But, we live in an age when it is virtually impossible to hear yourself think. We have more time saving devices than every generation that has gone before but the general noise of media, and distraction has made silent reflection very hard indeed. Wherever you are sitting right now, assuming you are in a public place, look around. How many people are looking at a smart phone? Constant engagement and noise. My wife describes this feeling as like having the M25, (the ring-road around London), in your head.

Modern life presents busy-ness as a norm. It is ever so easy to juggle credit card deals and search for voucher codes, and feel the need to stay on top of several social media accounts simultaneously, (WhatsApp, Messenger, Snap, Facebook, Text), but you do not have to. You do not have to attend three social events on the same evening or multitask between your online grocery shopping and work emails. Choose simplicity. It will create space and stillness on the inside and help you think and reflect clearly.

Habit three– Less Digital (sign off).

We all know this is true. Since 2007 we have become cyborgs. The internet in our pockets promised so much but has left us tired and never at rest.

"Technology can be our best friend, and technology can also be the biggest party pooper of our lives. It interrupts our own story, interrupts our ability to have a thought or a daydream, to imagine something wonderful, because we're too busy bridging the walk from the cafeteria back to the office on the cell phone." Steven Spielberg

As a family, we turn off all phones from five pm on a Friday for twenty four hours and we all unwind and slow down and become less frantic. We are not Amish, we just want technology to be our servant not our master. We also try to turn off our phones at eight pm on weekdays and they are off until seven am the next morning. The fact that we find this so hard is perhaps the evidence that smartphone addiction is real. Try it. My bet is that you would find giving up coffee easier.

Habit four - Solitude

Go for a walk (run) in nature <u>on your own</u> regularly. No podcast, music, phone calls – just you on your own with time to think. As with habit three above, it will feel most strange as silence may be a stranger to you but it is in the undistracted silence you are most likely to be able to hear yourself think.

C. We are changed by what we believe

Change happens because of what we believe and think. At some point, you may have pondered the question 'Why am I here?' or 'What is the meaning of my life?' As far as I am aware Hippos do not stand around at the bottom of lakes in Botswana asking such questions. It would appear to be a uniquely human thing. This is probably the emotive bit of this book because for so many of us faith and religion carry much baggage and often personal pain. In fact, in England where I live we are taught from a young age to never discuss money, religion or politics. We have made an exception recently due to Brexit.

People look to philosophy and faith to answer questions of meaning. I will not hope to address this question for you here as entire libraries of books exist around this subject alone but without an internal compass that points the ship of your life in a particular direction it is somewhat challenging to answer more granular specific questions like: 'what is the best thing I could do with my life'? It would be like giving you holiday recommendations without knowing whether you prefer the heat or cold, mountain adventure or sun lounger.

If you believe this is all there is and there is no God or moral authority outside of your own mind, and that we are just highly evolved mammals driven by instinct and a 'Selfish Gene', then the pursuit of pleasure and reproduction to pass on the aforementioned gene and an Epicurean lifestyle may seem a sensible way forward for you.

For the record, I mentor many people from all walks of life and it seems clear that such a lifestyle whilst promising pleasure does not appear to enable people to flourish and be the best version of themselves. On the contrary. It seems that the pursuit of pleasure as an end in itself can undermine the desire for purpose and meaning which often involves discomfort. I am sure you will have your own views on this. The main point being that our 'worldview' is incredibly important in shaping who we become and what we do.

If faith plays an important part in your life (I am a Christian), you may believe a loving and just God created you for a purpose and you are perfectly designed for that purpose. What you do with your life must be informed by your faith (or worldview) and you must surely choose a vocation that mirrors the things that please God. These might include love, mercy, kindness to others, etc. If what you do does not mirror what you believe you may become conflicted on the inside and may feel a lack integrity. This will lead to anxiety and stress.

If you are unsure as to what you believe which is the situation that so many of my friends find themselves in, then I do recommend you consider attending an Alpha Course which is a good way of exploring these things further and listening to others' points of view.

What one believes goes beyond your view of spirituality but also your definition of success, (is it about trying to accumulate more than others?), or is it about leaving a legacy that makes your grandchildren proud?

What you believe is all important in your journey of vocation and self-discovery and it is the third leg of the stool that will contribute to your transformation.

So, the three legs of the tripod are: what you believe about the world around you and your place in it, the things you do and do not do, (habits), and finally the people you spend most of your time with. These work together in symphony and shape who you become and therefore what you do.

Developing your vision

"You cannot live your life looking at yourself from someone else's point of view".
Penelope Cruz

This chapter is about vision.

In this book, Vision means what are you going to do with your life and why?

It is the ability to think about or plan the future with imagination or wisdom. It is the mental image of something we see in our mind's eye. In fact, when you think about anything at all, images come to mind. When I say Switzerland, maybe you picture a watch, chocolates or hopefully a mountain coated in the white stuff. Suppose you need to drive to your local supermarket later. Try to get there (without your TomTom) without first imagining the roads you need to drive along. I bet you cannot do it. We are very visual creatures. We think and reason in pictures.

Now, which images come to mind when I ask you what your future looks like? Or if I suggest imagining your life ten years from now, where are you? Who are you with? What cause burns in your heart, and how are you spending your time, treasure and talents? Vision is about imagining your future.

Hopefully, you are reading this book because you have already entertained the possibility that your future need not follow a set script handed to you by others. You know it is possible to make choices which result in a very different painting on the canvas of your life to that which has gone before. You get to pick the colours, the subject, and the process.

There are two common conversations I have had with people who are unclear about their vision. The first involves a fear of running in the wrong direction, and the second involves doing nothing at all. I want to suggest to you that inertia and apathy (the second risk), are more problematic than running in the wrong direction for a short time. Standing still because of uncertainty can lead to procrastination (a wait and see mentality), and procrastination can lead to laziness. Laziness is the enemy of all things noble.

Without a personal vision then there will be a vacuum in your life and someone else's vision will probably fill that void. You will be like a ship in the high seas without sails or rudder and visionary people around you will see that and in good faith will ask you to join in with their vision. Visionary leaders cannot help but recruit others into their vision. It is one of their greatest strengths. They may even do that to help you because they hate to see potential wasted and believe in you. You will probably say yes mainly because you cannot think of a good reason to say no, especially if their vision is noble.

You may have read or watched a play by Tom Stoppard called Rosencrantz and Guildenstern Are Dead. In Shakespeare's Hamlet play, Rosencrantz and Guildenstern are the most insignificant people, old school friends, summoned by King Claudius to probe Hamlet's bizarre behaviour. In Stoppard's play, Rosencrantz and Guildenstern become the central characters while the Hamlet figures become mere plot devices. The play becomes the story of two ordinary men caught up in events they could neither understand nor control. For them, their fate was sealed because Shakespeare had already predestined their end. They were a play within a play. They were not free at all. These fatalistic words are spoken:

"We're actors — we're the opposite of people."

And

"Audiences know what to expect, and that is all that they are prepared to believe in."

Tom Stoppard, Rosencrantz and Guildenstern Are Dead

Maybe you can relate to the feeling of being caught up in someone else's 'play' and being bound by expectations from which it is not easy to escape.

This play touches something in the audience at a deep level. Are we free? Do we have the power to shape our destiny and choose a path? Can we really weave our own tapestries with the threads life has thrown at us? Or has that already been scripted for us? These questions can be answered philosophically, spiritually and sociologically and I do not intend to explore these in this book.

I think we all know that we are made to be more than actors in someone else's play, or dispensable pieces on someone else's chessboard.

The only antidote to this is to have a personal vision to steer what you do and why. Not that your vision cannot align perfectly with that of another person, or that I am advocating an individualistic approach to life. Rather, that unless you learn to say 'no' to some things, what you say 'yes' to will lack bandwidth and therefore impact. Collaborate with others but do so because it is your vision and in your power to do so.

The world-famous investor Warren Buffett once gave a lecture at a university and he recommended to the students that to have a fruitful life they follow three steps.

Step One. Write a list of twenty five things important to you in your life, (family, work, friends, holidays, pets, skiing, learning Japanese etc)

Step two. Order the list of twenty five things so that the most important is at the top and the least important at the bottom.

Step three. Delete the bottom twenty from the list and just give all that saved time to the top five and do them well.

It is a simple exercise but makes a powerful point. We need to know what is important to us and do those things well or we may do all twenty five things badly.

So, my first point is that you need to have a vision and without it, you will probably live someone else's vision for you which will be out of tune with who you are inside. Or as the actress, Penelope Cruz helpfully stated:

"You cannot live your life looking at yourself from someone else's point of view".

You are to have your own voice, not echo the words and sentiment of another.

Now onto the common fear of running in the wrong direction. For me, this has probably been the single biggest challenge. The fear looks like something along these lines:

"Unless I am one hundred percent certain about this new possibility I may actually run in the wrong direction and not be available when the right thing comes along".

The real question here is whether we are allowed to be agile and opportunistic whilst searching for one's life's calling. I want to suggest the answer is yes.

A friend and mentor, Rob Scott-Cook once said to me:

"Do not worry too much about the destination, just make sure you are comfortable with the direction".

That has been enormously helpful. None of us know what the future holds. Life throws curve balls at us financially, in health and a range of circumstances outside of our control. There are limitations which we must learn to embrace as they are our reality. We ignore reality at our peril. But, in exploring new directions you will find you need to test new waters and try some new things. This brings us neatly onto investing in personal research and development.

Research & Development

"I have not failed. I've just found 10,000 ways that won't work."
Thomas Edison

In your quest for a Life Pivot you will need to conduct some personal research and development. It is a bit like a Russian doll set where you lift out the first doll only to reveal a doll beneath that, and one beneath that and so on. Discovering what you could and should do with the rest of your life to be fruitful; and fulfilled is a journey of self-discovery. I have already talked about understanding your gifts, passions and skills and I also have written about how helpful knowing your weaknesses and limitations can be.

This chapter looks at gleaning some perspective from industry. Big brands you know well spend billions each year on researching and developing new products and ideas for their future. It is typically between 5-15% of their annual sales. You may recall that Google was famous for insisting that all its employees spend one day a week on a personal idea. The goal was to retain their innovative culture and whilst that day may be wasted in many instances, they knew they would hit the jackpot every now and then with things like Gmail. Known for pursuing moon-shot research and development projects, the Mountain View, Californian based internet company has invested in seemingly outlandish technologies such as self-driving cars (Waymo), computer eyewear and balloon-distributed Wi-Fi. The company employs about 18,600 people in research and development.

If you are a Netflix customer you will know that Netflix originals is the strategy through which Netflix produces its own content such as House of Cards and Designated Survivor. It all begins with a 'Pilot'. This is typically a one hour sample of the proposed series which is released and then customers have the opportunity to like, dislike, watch or ignore. Based on the response the company will either go on to create a multi-year series or bin it.

Why am I writing about Netflix in a book about vocation? It is a simple idea and one worth making clearly. If these companies believe they should spend ten to twenty percent of their resources on exploring their possible 'futures' should you not also spend your resource on exploring your possible futures? For most of us that looks like between half a day and a full day a week exploring new things.

One of the problems identified in the chapters on Gifts and Passions was that we simply no longer know ourselves. Most people I speak to cannot say what they are gifted and passionate about. Often they project what they would like their answer to be. Part of the reason for this is that we are prone to living narrow, (notice I did not say shallow) existences. Our education system takes us in aged five and pops us out aged sixteen or eighteen, and for many it is straight onto the next conveyor belt of university, and then onto a graduate training scheme, or first job and the rest just seems to happen as more of a progression of events rather than by affirmative decision. This necessarily means that there are questions we do not ask, options we do not consider and assumptions we make.

If you know there is something else for you out there, how do you go about finding it? Surely, it needs to, one way or another, come out of new experiences whether that is in the context of work or a hobby?

Personal Research & Development is a bit like speed dating with ideas and vocation. It gives you the chance to meet different people, with different worldviews, approaches and even if 'the shoe does not fit', it is still a useful exercise because it stimulates your own thinking. Why did it not fit? What did you not like about it, and what would you prefer? These are all helpful indicators.

As Thomas A. Edison said concerning his invention:

"I have not failed. I've just found 10,000 ways that won't work."

Edison even saw the dead ends as helpful answers. What he heard was "do not go down that road again".

After I sold my first online legal business, I experienced an uncomfortable vacuum. I was determined to find a new vision and contribute to the world around me once again.

My own research and development included:

a. Running entrepreneurial workshops for charities in Africa. At one point we could have moved to Cape Town to work with transformational businesses.
b. Exploring whether I could acquire and/or develop a business in South Africa to provide economic sustainability to a charity I knew supporting children at risk,
c. Mentoring entrepreneurs (especially those making social impact) and establishing a Bristol meet-up especially for those interested in social impact;
d. Investing in other start-ups and providing some encouragement and coaching;
e. Providing support to a social enterprise helping ex-offenders. It involved a discussion about whether we could make chicken coops in a prison to sell in the UK and provide carpentry skills, sustainability etc.
f. Mentoring generally;
g. Horticulture.

The list goes on. They were all done in good faith and with each opportunity I was asking the deep question "is this my next thing'? Honestly, it was exhausting.

I draw on many years of experience as an entrepreneur. I learned that agility was the biggest asset. There is a common joke among the entrepreneurs I know that business plans are worthless, but the planning is indispensable. The plans never work out, and those who succeed change their business plans on a weekly basis for the first year or two. It is just part of the journey.

When starting a new thing, all one has is an idea and a set of unproven assumptions which could be true or false. This is the reason eighty percent of start-ups fail in year one and only half of those exist five years later. The entrepreneur's job is to launch the simplest version of their product as soon as possible and test their assumptions. Is there a need for it? Will people pay? Does it solve a problem? And with the feedback, the entrepreneur learns and then changes their original idea so it becomes what it needs to be in order to flourish. Or, as is often the case, the original idea is dropped in favour of something better that the entrepreneur would not have discovered but for the painful launch and learning cycle. Did you know YouTube was originally a dating app? It is true… and their 'failures' resulted in something far more significant.

The process of learning involves trying new things, paying attention and then based on what you learn trying something else. It is not a case of finding one carefully calibrated answer to all questions and delivering that one solution. Rather, it is a process of refinement whereby you become far more self-aware though the five questions and tools I outline in this book and then use them as a filter to guide you. Even then you will be learning and tweaking as you go as set out in the diagram below.

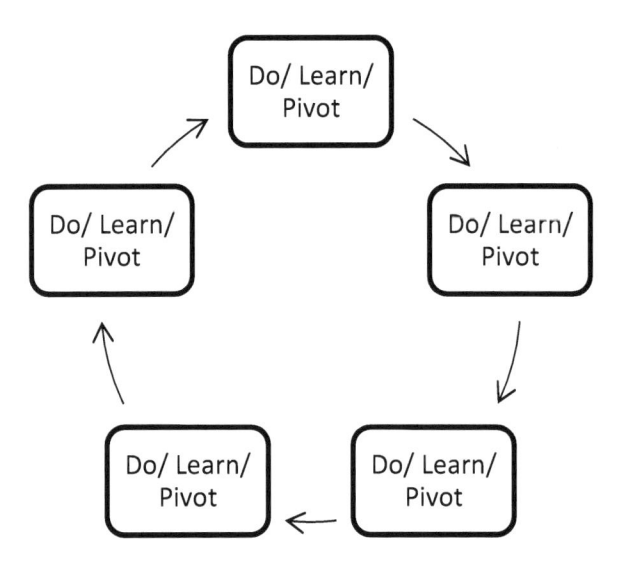

```
        Do/ Learn/
         Pivot
    ↗              ↘
Do/ Learn/      Do/ Learn/
  Pivot           Pivot
    ↑              ↓
Do/ Learn/  ←   Do/ Learn/
  Pivot           Pivot
```

I, therefore, want to suggest to you that doing nothing, and waiting for a true vocation and vision to fall out of the sky, is a bad idea as it may never happen. Rather, pick a general direction (even without a destination in mind) that mirrors your gifts, passions, values, and personality and start walking one step at a time and be ready for a big pivot into your true vocation along the way. Or as some say, you can only change the direction of a ship that is moving.

Like me, you may have 'Googled' the subject of vision and found five step programmes designed to draft a personal vision/mission statement but I am afraid human beings are too complex and multifaceted to provide easy answers to such weighty questions. Try them out, but honestly, I cannot even tell you whether I prefer my eggs poached or scrambled. In fact, as I hope this book has illustrated, this process is more akin to an archaeological dig than a five step questionnaire because you and me are unique. That is a great thing.

For me, my pivot was a process not an event. It took many years. There have not been lightbulb moments, and I have often feared it was one giant wild goose chase. But, in fact, rather than having a Eureka moment it has been like doing a five hundred piece puzzle where the edges were identifiable (the edges being the 'truth about me statements), but the picture inside was not. As I added pieces to the jigsaw (through experiences, observations, conversations, and reflection) the picture began to take shape.

Vision is a direction, not a destination. It is a journey, not an event. It is a picture of the future you imagine but it changes the more you look at it. It is more of a 'why?' than a 'what?'

Leaving the Shire

Well done for reading this far. This question of a life pivot, calling, purpose, meaning, living passionately, fruitfulness or however you wish to describe it has fascinated me for years. Partly because it is what I want for me but also because it comes up in conversation all the time with people I meet. Maybe, just maybe, there is a new script, and future which I was put on this planet for? Maybe it is not entirely mystical but something hidden in plain sight to be unearthed and lived? A precious raw material inside of each of us to be mined.

Everything you have read and reflected on comes to nothing unless you now have the 'oomph' to get up and go.

Question: What would you do next in your life having reflected on your unique gifts, passions, skills, weaknesses, personality type, and motivations, if you were not afraid?

Pause for thought.

One of the biggest causes of inertia for me has been the fear of running passionately in the wrong direction. We all know that thinking new thoughts translate into action at some point, but what action? I am so conscious of how many cul-de-sacs I have been into as part of my own Research and Development.

But I am relieved that I did not put all my eggs into any one of those baskets as I could have ended up further downstream from where I started. Have you ever had a similar thought?

A second thing that has caused inactivity on my part is a lack of confidence in my own conclusions. I now know my coordinates and general direction but what happens if in three years I go through this exercise and get entirely different answers?

These are the chief barriers to progress in my view. How does one overcome these legitimate mental blockades? I suspect the answer lies in taking your emerging truth statements about you, into the real world. In the world of Silicon Valley they describe this as the release of the beta version.

A new app, or product is put into the hands of others and a process of feedback, learning and reiterations begins which leads to the refining of the original version. This is probably true in this process as well. If you wait until you are one hundred percent certain about what makes you tick on all six points I identified, there is a distinct probability that you will never see change happen.

Warren Buffet once said concerning his assessments of things:

"I would rather be vaguely right than precisely wrong".

Step one - Make a choice.

You do not have to do anything. You are free. But an invitation awaits for you to become the best version of who you are. The reason you have read this book, messaged friends and discussed these issues with those closest to you is that you desire change. It may be a tweak in what you do or the way you do it but for some it will be more of a U-Turn. At some point you just need to make a decision and say "yes, that is me, I am going to start moving in a new direction even if it is only one step today".

Jeff Bezos, the founder of Amazon in his 2010 Princetown speech said:

"How will you use your gifts? What choices will you make?

Will inertia be your guide, or will you follow your passions?

Will you follow dogma, or will you be original?

Will you choose a life of ease, or a life of service and adventure?

Will you wilt under criticism, or will you follow your convictions?

Will you bluff it out when you're wrong, or will you apologize?

Will you guard your heart against rejection, or will you act when you fall in love?

Will you play it safe, or will you be a little bit swashbuckling?

When it's tough, will you give up, or will you be relentless?

Will you be a cynic, or will you be a builder?

Will you be clever at the expense of others, or will you be kind?

I will hazard a prediction. When you are 80 years old, and in a quiet moment of reflection narrating for only yourself the most personal version of your life story, the telling that will be most compact and meaningful will be the series of choices you have made. In the end, we are our choices."

In some ways we need someone to say that to us every day. Each day holds new possibilities.

We are our choices. What choices might you make today?

I do not like running, but a few years ago my friend and I discussed running a full marathon from Bristol to Bath. We do not love running by any means but it seemed to us to be a great goal and something to tick off the 'bucket list'. After running a 10k we sat down and simply paid our £35 and entered. Did that step prepare us for the 26.2 miles, or contribute to the eventual completion of that race? No it did not, but it was a line in the sand we both stepped across and it forced us to take simple steps, (lots of them) in the right direction. These steps included new running shoes, a training schedule, and a better diet (less carbs). It was the moment of choice and passing the finishing line together became an inevitable outcome.

This first step is therefore about taking first steps. It is all too easy to read the stories of inspirational individuals who have overcome the odds and done tremendous things and miss the fact that they did not know the end of their story at the beginning of their story. Rather, they took a simple step which led to a second step, which then led to a third step and so forth. This is the story of George and Carolyn Snyman of Hands at Work whose first step was to join Hezekiah on his community visits so they could see something new. That first step became the catalyst to an entire movement.

Step two – Start off with Passion

Knowing one's passion is just one of the five coordinates in this book but I think it is the best place to start. Gifts, skills and personality can fit into your passion but not vice versa.

The purpose of the five steps in this book is not to give you a destination but rather to provide direction. Perhaps for most of us the outcome of the journey is unlikely to be a movement or a global organisation but a new way of looking at things. A new perspective on what is important and what is not. This means that you are more likely to know what kind of person you want and need to be, rather than what specific jobs you should be doing. This is because what we do comes out of who we are.

There will inevitably be a 'what?' but in order for you to flourish, you need to really care about what you are doing or you will not keep going. In his book Michelangelo famously said:

"Your gifts lie in the place where your values, passions and strengths meet. Discovering that place is the first step toward sculpting your masterpiece. Your Life."

This is the challenge that lies ahead for each of us. We are not to simply tick six boxes but rather we need to add them all to the mixing bowl and allow them to interweave into the tapestry of each one of us. No two tapestries will look alike and comparing ourselves to other people is fruitless.

Once you have an inkling as to the direction in which you are travelling, what matters then is to leave your comfort zone and start your journey.

Step three– Get out there

I cannot write about living in a bubble without the film 'The Truman Show' starring Jim Carey coming to mind. Truman lives in a manufactured world which is in fact a reality TV set and he aches for something real in the same way that Rosencrantz and Guildenstern are unable to guide destiny because there is an invisible hand of a director behind the scenes. Truman eventually faces his fears and sails across the fake ocean and breaks out of the set into his real life. Interestingly, for Truman it was fear that kept him captive in the reality TV show and love that set him free.

Fortunately, our lives are not a reality TV set and we do get to make choices. However, we can live in a bubble much like Truman because we have made it that way. Whilst we can point to 'scripts' in our lives which have sent us down the wrong road, we have all too often played along.

There comes a time in life when it seems change happens less and there is an equilibrium of sorts which takes over. We end up being surrounded by people, things and experiences which mirror our own past choices. It is not a criticism; we have a cognitive bias to do this. But, what this means is in a season of pursuing change it is that much harder to encounter different ideas, ideas that might kick start something in us. As the famous Zoologist Jane Goodall said,

"Change happens by listening and then starting a dialogue with the people who are doing something you do not believe is right."

When did you last have a conversation with someone whose perspectives and experiences were so different to your own that you left questioning your own ideas?

Am I willing to be open to new ideas and new ways of doing and seeing things?

Let me give a real life example of an entrepreneurial idea that I have wrestled with for some time: A peer to peer kitchen platform. Think Airbnb for food. Food delivery is globally scaling into a multi trillion industry and it is all picked up from commercial kitchens.

Yes, I know you may not be in business at all. The example to follow could equally be something related to re-training as a teacher, or something utterly altruistic. But, as this is my book I will give an example that mirrors my wiring.

Why, is it not possible to order food from other people in my community (neighbours)? The best Green Thai Curry may be found in a Thai restaurant but equally it may be found elsewhere, in the kitchen of someone who has recently moved from Thailand. This idea could remove overheads, engage community eating, foster new relationships and put pounds or dollars into the pockets of people living in the community. Good idea? This is not Dragons Den or Shark Tank, but I wanted to share the type of thing I come up with after my second coffee in the morning.

Where did this come from? First of all I am aware of the macro trend known as the sharing economy and namely Airbnb. I love what it has accomplished especially for individuals who are making extra income. Secondly, I know that people order food en masse and that delivery is not being managed by the restaurants but by third parties like Deliveroo. And finally, the true driver that got me thinking in this way is the terrible food poverty in my city and beyond and the fact that many do not know how to cook and therefore order take-away which is expensive and not always nourishing.

My thought, was, how hard would it be for some individuals I know to cook two lasagnes instead of one, and then sell them at a lower cost to others nearby? Who knows, using such an infrastructure may even allow for communities to feed one another, teach cooking, and address the problem of obesity in our country which is costing our health service north of £26 billion per annum.

This idea came about by joining various dots. But as of now it has gone no further because:

a) I am not a chef or caterer and know little about the regulations;
b) I feel ill equipped compared to the guys behind Airbnb;
c) I am not a politician and do not have a good understanding of food poverty, its causes and solutions.

In other words due to my perceived deficiencies from my current world, I turn away from something that could make a real contribution and societal impact.

Using this reasoning, I should really just get involved in more of what I have done historically, however unfulfilling. That clearly does not 'scratch the itch' or I would not be asking such questions in the first place.

I believe the answer is for you and me (like Truman) to leave our familiar surroundings and in the example above go and meet people who are in closer proximity to the problem and opportunity and build new relationships and learn. Who knows, I may hold a key to a lock they hold and vice versa.

The second part of this puzzle is that we do not need to go it alone.

There is an old African proverb that says:

'If you want to go fast, go alone. If you want to go far, go together.'

If like me you feel you need to be the complete article already, life just does not work that way. So many of the people I meet have learned to rely on other people. In fact the greatest entrepreneurs I know personally have a single strength in knowing how to spot talent in others. They know they cannot go it alone.

I therefore invite you to join me in stepping into the unknown. For me and my idea above, that would look like meeting people who work with food banks and deal with these challenges on a day to day basis.

My friend Jamie is a successful entrepreneur and recently sold his business. Everything about him was already adventurous so this came as no surprise to me, but since the age of sixteen he has loved keeping bees. He has pivoted his career into becoming a commercial bee keeper and now has over three hundred hives.

He did not have any land, or any hives, or anyone who said they wanted to buy honey from him but he immersed himself in that world and visited leading bee keepers in Finland and elsewhere and made lots of friends along the way. Waggle and Hum was born.

Will the end product be honey, wax, honey gin, or mead? Who knows, but this is an example of someone taking bold steps and not waiting until all the dots line up. It is something he is passionate about, he is good at business and with people, so watch this space.

It is difficult to suggest how you might try new things and meet new people, but it will probably involve different demographics, and zip/post codes. To avoid accidental bias, start by researching a list of people and organisations who already care about the thing you are passionate about (or at least have the seeds of passion for), and get to know them and offer to volunteer in their 'thing'.

The point of this step is that in the pursuance of change, clearly it will not be greatly enabled by doing all the same things you have previously done or currently do, in the same area with the same people.

Step four – Stand on the shoulders of giants

I touched on this already. A common fear and limitation is known as impostor's syndrome. In the world of entrepreneurship I come cross it constantly. I know two-three entrepreneurs who have each started and sold three-four businesses in the last ten years but they all still think they were lucky and are unlikely candidates for a next venture. That syndrome is certainly true for me.

There is an assumption that needs to be dismantled right now and that is that you need to be completely novel and a genius and do something that has never been done, or think thoughts that have never been thought. It simply is not true. If that is your benchmark, then quit now.

There are countless 'heroes' who have simply taken things one step forward with some incredible results.

Exhibit one – Steve Jobs

Steve Jobs – He did not invent the music player, the mouse, the touch screen or the computer but what he did do is 'reinvent' them. Former executive John-Louise Gassee wrote:

"Apple hasn't invented anything, but is more like a great chef. Their expertise lies in taking existing ingredients available to everyone and bringing them together into a delicious dish never imagined before."

Exhibit two – Sir Isaac Newton

Sir Isaac Newton was an English physicist, mathematician, astronomer, alchemist and inventor who wrote, concerning his own accomplishments:

"If I have seen further, it is by standing upon the shoulders of giants"

His point being that if he accomplished more than his peers and those scientists who went before him it was in the light of their discoveries that he was able to develop his own.

Exhibit three – Thomas Edison

Thomas A Edison – the inventor of the lightbulb amongst other things wrote:

I am more of a sponge than an inventor. I absorb ideas from every source. I take half-matured schemes for mechanical development and make them practical. I am a sort of middleman between the long-haired and impractical inventor and the hard-headed business man who measures all things in terms of dollars and cents. My principal business is giving commercial value to the brilliant but misdirected ideas of others."

I rest my case in true legal style. It is fine to rely on other people's thoughts and ideas and use them as scaffolding upon which you launch your own ideas, companies and movements. If these great people did it, we would be foolish to start from zero in the things we do.

Is it possible that in the light of your known passions, and unique capabilities that you can mix those together into the mixing bowls of other people's existing ingredients?

Turning back to my Airbnb for eating, do I need to own and know all the answers and hold all five hundred pieces of the puzzle or can I forge unlikely partnerships with other people and accelerate the vision? I think it is ok to take small steps in that direction and see where it leads.

This final chapter is the 'pep talk'. If this were Lord of the Rings this would be where I invite you to embark on a journey and leave the Shire. Write down the truth statements and pin them up somewhere and know that you are unique. Then take steps.

They do not need to be many in number but they do need to be in the correct direction. There will be a destination but the journey of being one hundred percent you is the reward and that is the greatest gift you can receive. And finally, my prayer is that you become all you were designed to be and in ten years look back on today having flourished beyond your wildest dreams.

Further Resources

Life Pivot Coaching & Mentoring Programme

If you would benefit from having someone support you during your Life Pivot and help you find clarity by asking you the important questions and identifying a clear plan of action then please contact Brad at:

www.LifePivot.co.uk

Can you please do something for me?

This Life Pivot book will hopefully evolve into something broader and deeper over time and I need your help. Please will you share your own Life Pivot stories with me so that our Life Pivot Community can learn together. We would love to hear from you.

'If you want to go fast, go alone. If you want to go far, go together.'

Join our Community - Engage/Share/Learn
Facebook: www.facebook.com/groups/LifePivot/
Twitter: @LifePivotBook
LinkedIn: www.linkedin.com/company/lifepivot/

Works Cited

I. www.Gallup.com. Report - State of the Global Workplace 2013.
II. Buffy the Vampire Slayer (1998). [Motion Picture]
III. Robinson, K., & Aronica, L. (2009). The element: How finding your passion changes everything. New York: Penguin Group USA.
IV. In Bloom, H. (1987). George Bernard Shaw's Saint Joan. New York: Chelsea House Publishers.
V. Palmer, P. J. (2000). Let your life speak: Listening for the voice of vocation. San Francisco: Jossey-Bass.
VI. KRUGER, J. AND DUNNING, D. Unskilled and unaware of it: How difficulties in recognizing one's own incompetence lead to inflated self-assessments. 1999 - Journal of Personality and Social Psychology
VII. William Shakespeare As You Like It, V. I
VIII. Briggs, Katharine C. Myers-Briggs Type Indicator. Form G. Palo Alto, Calif. :Consulting Psychologists Press, 1987.
IX. The road back to you : an Enneagram journey to self-discovery Ian Morgan Cron Downers Grove : IVP Books / InterVarsity Press, 2016

X.	The Wisdom of the Enneagram: Complete Guide to Psychological and Spiritual Growth for the Nine Personality Types Paperback – 30 Sep 1999 by Don Richard Riso
XI.	"The Psychology of Human Misjudgment" by Charlie Munger Harvard University 1995
XII.	Manning, B. (1990). The Ragamuffin Gospel: Embracing the unconditional love of God. Sisters, OR: Multnomah Books.
XIII.	Willimon, B., McCarthy, K., Huff, K., Fincher, D., Foley, J., Cleveland, R., Treem, Sony Pictures Home Entertainment (Firm),. (2013). House of cards: The complete first season
XIV.	Tolkien, J.R.R. The Fellowship of the Ring. New York: Houghton Mifflin Company, 1994
XV.	Lord Acton Letter 1887
XVI.	Ogden Actuarial Tables - Personal Injury and Fatal Accident Cases Prepared by an Inter-disciplinary Working Party of Actuaries, Lawyers, Accountants and other interested parties Seventh edition
XVII.	Jim Collins, Turning the Flywheel: A Monograph to Accompany Good to Great
XVIII.	Stoppard, Tom. Rosencrantz & Guildenstern Are Dead. New York :Grove Press, 1968.
XIX.	"If I have seen further, it is by standing upon the shoulders of giants" ... This quote is from a letter written to fellow scientist, Robert Hooke in February 1675
XX.	"Edison The Man And His Work" by George S. Bryan 192

Printed in Great
Britain
by Amazon